D0970391

THE GOOD
BREXITEER'S GUIDE
TO ENGLISH LIT

THE GOOD BREXITEER'S GUIDE TO ENGLISH LIT

John Sutherland

PREFACE by John Crace

REAKTION BOOKS LTD

in memoriam Monica Jones,
Brexitiste avant la lettre

Published by
REAKTION BOOKS LTD
Unit 32, Waterside
44–48 Wharf Road
London N1 7UX, UK
www.reaktionbooks.co.uk

First published 2018
Copyright © John Sutherland 2018
Copyright for the Preface © John Crace 2018

The right of John Sutherland to be identified as Author of this work
has been asserted by him in accordance with the Copyright,
Designs and Patents Acts 1988

All rights reserved

No part of this publication may be reproduced, stored in a retrieval system,
or transmitted, in any form or by any means, electronic, mechanical,
photocopying, recording or otherwise, without the prior permission
of the publishers

Printed and bound in Great Britain
by TJ International, Padstow, Cornwall

A catalogue record for this book is available from the British Library

ISBN 978 1 78023 992 7

Illustration on p. 16 courtesy of the British Cartoon Archive,
University of Kent

'Dust.'

– Philip Larkin's reply to the question why he never chose to holiday
on the Continent, in conversation with the author, *c.* 1966

'That jingoistic England that is trying to march us out of
the EU, that is the England I don't want to know.'

– John le Carré, in high disgust, CBS TV, 18 September 2017

CONTENTS

PREFACE by John Crace 11

INTRODUCTION 17

The Battle of Maldon 21

Domesday Book 26

The Tattooed Heart 30

Malory and King Arthur: The Literary Invention of England 32

The Literature of the People 41

The Bloudie Crosse 48

The Brexit Boadicea 49

Boadicea in Stone 56

Enter the Maybot, Clanking 58

Fee-Fi-Fo-Fum: I Smell the Blood of an Englishman! 59

Shakespeare: 'This England' 70

The Oxford Book of English Verse 76

School Songsters 82

Brexiteers, Buccaneers, Musketeers; or, 'Up Yours, Señors!' 86

Dickens, Anti-Brexiteer Extraordinaire 91

Our National Anthem 93

Gibbon: The Congenital British *Non Serviam* 97

Ivanhoe and the Norman Yoke 100

Jane Austen's 'England' 104

W. E. Henley 107

Rivers of Blood Wash over Our Green and Pleasant Land 111

Brexit's Green and Pleasant Land 118

A. E. Housman and Thomas Hardy 121

DNB/OED 125

Land of Hope and Glory 131

Orwell: Quarter-French, Wholly English 134

Rhodes Must Fall. Kipling Must Go. Buchan Goes On and On 137

Kipling Again 145

Nigel Farage's Favourite Novel 148

King Solomon's (Not Africa's) Mines 152

Lady Chatterley's Lover: 'Old England' is Gone Forever 154

The Amis Objection 160

Philip Larkin: The Greatest English Poet of Our Time 162

Why the Brexiteer Loves Sherlock 166

Mad Dogs and Englishmen (and Jeeves) 169

The End of Jeeves   173

Invasion by Immigration – From Calais, Mars or Wherever   175

Dracula: Illegal Immigrant   180

God Loves England (Does He Not?)   185

Flashman   191

Goldfinger   196

The Poison Cabinet   201

Lost Englands   205

Virginia Woolf's Farewell to England (and the World)   206

The Queen and I   211

The Children of Men   213

London Fields   214

England, England   216

Take to the Boats!   218

McEwan's Objection   222

Hail Hilary!   223

The Satanic Verses: 'Not English!'   227

Epilogue   231

REFERENCES   233

ACKNOWLEDGEMENTS   240

PREFACE

John Crace

John Sutherland is open about having voted for the United Kingdom to remain in the European Union. So this book could be seen as the ultimate work of self-sacrifice; to give the Brexiteers something they were never able to give themselves. Even during the referendum, Brexit was an atavistic set of competing interests. Some wanted to get rid of immigrants; some wanted to restore British sovereignty; some just wanted to give the political elites a kicking. Sutherland has given them all a cultural and literary hinterland around which they can unite and against which Brexit can be better understood.

The referendum brought what had until then been an internal squabble within the Conservative Party on to the national stage. If the intention had been to unite the country and to settle the question of Britain's membership of the European Union for good, it backfired spectacularly. The country's divisions were split open by the referendum campaign, and there have as yet been no signs of any healing.

Brexit has taken its toll on Westminster as well as on the United Kingdom. The usual everyday processes of running the country have all but stalled as successive governments try to make a success of Brexit – something that has so far proved beyond them. What we have often got instead has been politics played out as farce.

David Cameron gave up on day one, by choosing to resign the morning after the referendum. That triggered one of the most bizarre leadership elections of modern times. While all the other hopefuls took to the airwaves in the weeks following Cameron's departure, Theresa May managed to get away with saying almost nothing. Whether by accident or design, it was a stunning piece of political gamesmanship. One by one, her rivals eliminated themselves from the contest by saying something catastrophically stupid, until May was the last person standing. It was the first time in British history that someone had become prime minister by taking a vow of silence.

What was so effective in getting her through the doors of 10 Downing Street proved less helpful in keeping her there. A prime minister can't get away with saying nothing indefinitely, and eventually she had to try out a few phrases, the most common of which was 'Brexit means Brexit.' While a few of those who had been enthusiastic about Britain leaving the EU took 'Brexit means Brexit' as a sign of intelligent life, most of the rest of the country began to wonder if there was even less to May than met the eye.

When May began answering completely different questions from the ones she had been asked, in every interview, a few of us dared to think her brain might have been hacked and taken over by malware. Ask her what 'Brexit means Brexit' really meant and she would invariably whirr into inaction and say, 'I am determined to be focused . . . [she wasn't; she really wasn't] . . . on the things that the British people are determined for me to focus on.' The Maybot was born.

Things didn't really improve throughout the first eight months of May's time in office. First, her government lost its case in the Supreme Court over its refusal to allow Parliament a vote on triggering Article 50. May was not at all happy about this: Britain hadn't voted to take back control in the EU referendum only to allow the British Parliament to have a say in how the country was run. She appeared to be even more angry when the Labour Party chose to thwart 'the will of the people' by voting with the government to trigger Article 50. Logic never was the Maybot's strong point.

Despite all these very obvious shortcomings, the Conservatives still held a twenty-point lead over Labour in the opinion polls, and immediately after the Easter break in 2017, May announced that she would be holding a snap general election – despite having explicitly stated on seven previous occasions that it wasn't in the national interest to hold a general election. Some people began to wonder if the Maybot were becoming confused between what was in the public interest and what was in her own.

The early weeks of the election campaign were characterized by Theresa May going round the country saying 'Strong and Stable' in front of a small group of Conservative Party activists who had been herded into one corner of a community centre to make it look on TV as if she were playing to sell-out audiences everywhere. Things didn't improve with the launch of her manifesto. Within days she was forced to insist that 'Nothing has Changed' as she changed pretty much everything.

May couldn't for the life of her see why everyone was calling her dementia tax a tax on dementia just because it was a tax that targeted people with dementia. Besides, her manifesto had never been meant to be seen as electoral promises; rather, it was just a series of random ideas formed of random sentences. It was around this time that even her advisers started calling her 'The Maybot'. The name seemed to describe her perfectly: awkward, lacking in empathy and – above all – not very competent.

Despite all this, the Conservatives still held a large lead going into polling day, and May expected to gain a sixty-to-eighty-seat majority. But the electorate saw things differently. Having been asked to back the prime minister and give her a strong mandate, they instead chose to give her no overall majority. The Maybot was devastated and the Tory Party far from impressed. Ordinarily, she would have been forced to go as leader within a week, but these were desperate times. The gene pool of talent within the party was so small that there were no obvious replacements. Besides, the last thing the Conservatives wanted was another election, as they would probably lose. So May's punishment for failure was being forced to stay on as prime minister.

Over the summer May lay low, licking her wounds and hoping no one in her party would launch a leadership bid against her. Come the party conference in October, she was ready to reboot herself. Only Maybot 2.0 looked to all intents and purposes much like Maybot 1.0. She had meant to convince the party that she had learned from her mistakes, but her apology for her election campaign, being too scripted, just sounded . . . too scripted. The comedian Simon Brodkin made his way to the stage to give May her P45 – which she accepted, because deep down that's what she really wanted. Then her voice went into revolt and refused to speak. The nadir was the frog leaping out of her throat and on to the screen behind her, where it started knocking off the slogans. 'Strong and Stable' became 'Rong and Stale'.

Then May realized that maybe it had been a mistake to leave David Davis in charge of the negotiations. Having told a select committee that his department had been making in-depth impact assessments on 58 sectors of the economy, the Brexit secretary was forced to admit that the assessments did not actually exist when he was asked to produce them. At this point May headed over to Brussels to take charge of the negotiations. Unfortunately, she had forgotten to inform Arlene Foster, the leader of the Democratic Unionist Party in Northern Ireland – on which she relied for her majority – and was then forced to tell the EU that she wasn't able to agree to the deal she had come over specially to sign.

Eventually the EU took pity and came to May's rescue. Better to deal with a fatally wounded Maybot whom they could at least vaguely trust, than risk her being sacked by the Tories and replaced with someone even more incompetent. So the EU signed off the first phase of the negotiations – even though no one could quite agree on what had been agreed – and gave the green light to the second phase.

The Maybot momentarily forgot that three members of her cabinet had been forced to resign, that the National Health Service was in crisis and that UK productivity was among the lowest of all G20 countries, and celebrated as if she had won the lottery. The British public, and her own parliamentary party, were less forgiving. Long before the second phase of negotiations had even begun, many in her own party were once more having serious doubts over her leadership skills. By February 2018 she was hanging on by her fingertips.

Brexit had done for one prime minister and dealt a fatal blow to another. Given time, it might even see off May's successor. There was one bright side for them, however. Now they would have the time to read John Sutherland's book and try to work out exactly where they had gone wrong.

"VERY WELL , ALONE "

VERY WELL, ALONE. David Low's post-Dunkirk cartoon.
Evening Standard, 18 June 1940.

INTRODUCTION

What happened to Britain – more specifically, England – on 24 June 2016 is routinely portrayed as the voice of the 'people' making itself heard like a thunderclap. Call it Brexit. It's a word that did not previously exist in the political lexicon which has served British parliamentary democracy for half a millennium. The *Oxford English Dictionary* records the arrival of the neologism in 2012, in a blog by Peter Wilding (neologisms everywhere). Wilding should have trademarked his invention: he would by now have made it to the *Sunday Times* rich list, so universal has the B-word become in public discourse.

What has been visible every day since midsummer 2016 is that Brexit has jolted us to a different place nationally, a place where even the most familiar things look suddenly unstable. What, for example, does the red postal pillar box, that wonderfully Trollopian, archetypally English, monarch-emblazoned innovation, mean after the referendum? Is its Englishness somehow restored?

What does Trollope himself mean in this new world? There is, of course, no question of how the Chronicler of Barsetshire would have cast his vote: the same way as Waltham Cross, where his home was. Leave!

There is little point in looking to the newspaper pundits for wisdom. The chicken entrails they scrutinized all proved wrong. They simply never saw Brexit coming. 'Oops', was the universal response from the wise ones, our so-called opinion-formers.

Why, though, this book?

Brexit, despite its referendum victory, is peculiarly hollow. It is an idea without political apparatus, without sustaining history, without field-tested ideology. Without thinkers. And without old-fashioned electoral appeal – except in the one-off, one-issue referendum. It and its chaotic party, the UK Independence Party 'Kippers', have twice fared little better at the polls than did the much-loved and other peculiarly British institution the Monster Raving Loony Party.

On the night of 8 June 2017, with the total failure of its electoral campaign, Brexit exploded, like a firework rocket, into sparkles. Yet even without MPs it was a force that had shaken England to its roots and would, quite probably, disunite the United Kingdom, for ill or good (I put it that way round because I voted Remain).

UKIP and its Brexit offspring came into the world, like newborns, with no thoughts, only reflexes (such as 'immigration/ nasty; nipple/nice'). As a party, or movement, it still twitches galvanically and calls its twitches policy. It is like Frankenstein's monster waiting for the lightning bolt.

Brexit has no intellectual history; no Disraeli to formulate a presiding idea equivalent to the one-nation Toryism Dizzy promulgated.[1] Neither does it have a body of inherited doctrine such as the so-called Marx-and-water which created the undestructive British version of Socialism, which in turn led to the creation of the post-war welfare state which lost its way under New Labour and is now riding off into Stalin and water. Because it possesses no guiding (or misguiding) ideology, Brexit constantly tears itself apart, looking inside itself for what it is all about. The Union Jack, to paraphrase Nietzsche, is not an argument.[2]

The aim of this short guide through a politically relevant side road of English literature is not to sneer, denounce, rant or satirize. I voted Remain and still believe that what happened on the night of 23 June 2016 was a wrong turn for my country. But I feel – who doesn't? – the raw power of Brexit. What did the *Daily Mail* call it, with a pragmatically misapplied Ibsen phrase? 'The Will of the People'. I respect Brexit's wilfulness, its muscle and its achievement. It has changed Britain. But I also see that gaping black hole where doctrine – call it 'thought' – should be.

I am a higher education teacher by profession, and this book offers a curriculum with some suggested stuffing for that ideological vacuity at the heart of the Brexit cause. I have quarried the great minds of the English past to put together this reading list. Call it food for thought. Much of it centres on the shadowy 'England' the Brexiteers revere, but never quite see clearly through the fog of their own mythologies. 'England' is a very complex notion.

It is clear that in what follows I'm loose in defining 'England', 'Britain' and 'UK'. Despite its name (United Kingdom Independence Party), the soul of the Brexit movement is, it strikes me, as English as the fry-up breakfast named English (which no other nation can bring itself to relish first thing in the morning). In this book I think, as best I can, about what England meant, means and will mean, and pass those thoughts on.

I have chosen literary minds, and highly literate minds, because those are what I know best and revere most. I believe literature is the most subtle and clever of the discourses the human race has created to understand itself and convey that understanding to others. I also believe that great literature has a shaping influence on the world.[3]

What follows, then, is a curriculum. I calculate that the literary works I have assembled, more or less chronologically, would furnish a year's study for a BA Honours degree in Brexit-related literature at a university. I have quoted lavishly along the way because I want this book to serve as something of an anthology, as well as a guide. Something, that is, to enjoy as well as think about.

The Battle of Maldon

The nuclear core of UKIP is anxiety about invasion. Invasion, that is, by foreigners, aliens, the 'other'. One of the most potent – and contentious – items in the Leave campaign was a vast poster entitled 'Breaking Point', depicting Nigel Farage, in 'they shall not pass' mode, standing in front of an apparently endless line of foreigners massing, the implied narrative suggested, to burst across the border. And go where? To the heart of England's Green and Pleasant Land. The 'swamping' that Margaret Thatcher direly feared in 1978 would come true, and how would the Iron Lady have voted in the referendum? Probably Leave.

Follow the thread and it takes us back to *The Battle of Maldon*, one of English literature's two most venerable surviving texts (forget *Beowulf*, the other one. The hero of that epic is a Swedish immigrant and the poem was written down, and 'improved', by Europhile – Romanist – monks).

UKIP should hold its annual conference (assuming it still has any existence as a party) on the muddy Blackwater estuary of the little town of Maldon, Essex, and make a reverential trip to the Maeldune Heritage Centre, where Humphrey Spender's magnificent 13-metre (42-ft) embroidery commemorating the battle resides.[4] This great English (stress that word) work of art was completed for the 1,000th anniversary of the battle, in 1991. Many Maldonian knitters pitched in with their needles flashing, one might fantasize, like Lilliputian swords, still drawn against the bastard Viking invader.

I came to know Humphrey well when I was writing the life of his brother the poet Stephen Spender in 2004. Humphrey confided that the concept of his great embroidery was that it should be an 'English' retort against that wretched triumphalist drape celebrating the Franco-Norman Conquest, the Bayeux Tapestry. Bear in mind that the Normans ('Northmen') were, aboriginally, Vikings. During the referendum campaign Nigel Farage liked to sport a tie depicting the Bayeux 'tapestry', to recall, as he mischievously said, 'the last time we were invaded and taken over'. His levity (he's a genuinely witty man) worked well against the gloomy Remoaners' 'Project Fear'. Black ties for them.

The fragmentary nine-hundred-odd lines of undated *The Battle of Maldon*, which have survived the ages, can be read as a proto-Brexit anthem. The poem commemorates what is, for us today, the old, old story: Britain being bled dry by foreigners. First comes the sword, then comes the tax demand: £350 million a week.

Vikings in longboats rolled up, year in year out, as regular as 6 April, demanding exorbitant annual taxes ('Danegeld', as it would later be called) in the form of gold rings, bars of silver, ornate spears and other treasure to take back to their windy corner of Europe. They would knock down a church or two in the process, and violate any local women who took their fancy. They had been doing it since who could remember when. Easy pickings. If one of the wounded were left alive, he would be flayed by the infuriated Anglo-Saxons, and his skin hung on the nearest church door. Barnier beware.

Byrhtnoth, an earl of the 'mad as hell and not going to take it any more' kind, finally resolved to make a stand for England, in the mud. No one is sure exactly where he stood. My good friend the place-name expert John Dodgson used to take groups of gumbooted Anglo-Saxon students annually over vast expanses of mud on the Maldon shore, speculating learnedly about the site of the fight and reciting the poem, to the amazement of locals. They would then wassail in the local mead hall (John liked his jar).

English resistance proved a big mistake. The Vikings invaded en masse, by way of reprisal, and had by far the better tactics: they were warriors. Byrhtnoth had at his command farmers who were handier with the hoe than with the broadsword; Danskers ate Anglo-Saxons for breakfast, and then had their wicked way with Mrs Anglo-Saxon for lunch.

After valiantly doing battle, Byrhtnoth was slain (chiefs are never merely 'killed'). The English know theirs is a lost cause, but, as the poem asserts so beautifully, the moral victory is theirs. An old thegn (beautiful word), Byrhtwold, loyal to the death, proclaims: 'Mind must be the stronger, heart the bolder,/ courage must be the greater, as our might lessens.' It rolls wonderfully off the tongue in the Anglo-Saxon (why on earth did we English stop speaking it? Let's bring it back after the final Brexit victory, as the Welsh have done with their language since devolution):

> *Byrhtwold maþelode,   bord hafenode*
> *(se wæs eald geneat),   æsc acwehte.*
> *He ful baldlice   beornas lærde:*
> *Hige sceal þe heardra,   heorte þe cenre,*
> *mod sceal þe mare,   þe ure mægen lytlað.*
> *Her lið ure ealdor   eall forheawen,*
> *god on greote.   A mæg gnornian*
> *se ðe nu fram þis wigplegan   wendan þenceð.*
> *Ic eom frod feores;   fram ic ne wille,*
> *ac ic me be healfe   minum hlaforde,*
> *be swa leofan men,   licgan þence.'*
> *Swa hi Æþelgares bearn   ealle bylde,*
> *Godric to guþe.   Oft he gar forlet,*
> *wælspere windan   on þa wicingas,*

> *swa he on þam folce   fyrmeſt eode,*
> *heow and hynde –   oðþæt he on hilde gecranc.*
> *Næs þæt na se Godric   þe ða guðe forbeah.*

Byrhtwold is then chopped into little pieces, as is his beloved ring-giver.[5]

The defeat was salutary. After the battle, ready for once in his reign, King Ethelred (nicknamed the 'Unready', son of King Edgar the Peaceful) undertook to pay the Vikings 10,000 Roman pounds (3,300 kg) in silver. As Wikipedia tells us, 'it is the first example of Danegeld in England.' Think £350-million-a-week Danegeld, AD 2016. What couldn't the British leper colonies have done with that ten grand (Roman)?

Bluntly, the Anglo-Saxons lost. But those valiant English Kippers *avant la lettre* embody (even minced up like sausage meat) that sense of being what Leonard Cohen called 'beautiful losers'. Their hearts are stronger because the battle was lost. We should remind ourselves of what the poet Arthur Hugh Clough wrote, in the same spirit, 1,000 years later:

> Say not the ſtruggle nought availeth,
>   The labour and the wounds are vain,
> The enemy faints not, nor faileth,
>   And as things have been they remain.

Losing, the Good Brexiteer avers, makes the losing Anglo-Saxons' point. UKIP did and does not expect, even after 23 June 2016, ever to be a government. It didn't, for God's sake, even expect to win the referendum. Farage conceded defeat, with a noble, Byrhtnothian air, while the votes were being counted: 'It's been an extraordinary referendum campaign, turnout looks to be exceptionally high and looks like Remain will edge it. UKIP and I are going nowhere and the party will only continue to grow stronger in the future.' It was political *ejaculatio praecox*, since Leave won thumpingly. An extraordinary referendum indeed.

There is something wonderfully Godot-like in UKIP's subsequent one member in Parliament (the 'Party'), who then resigns. Why? Independence does not compromise, even if that independence means extinction. The idea will live on, like that of Protestantism in England, where only 2 per cent of the population attend church.

MORAL: Losing proves that you may well be right.

Postscript: 'Danegeld'

The payment made to the victorious Danes following the Battle of Maldon, an annual tax, rose to ten times that amount in 1016. Such an outrageous amount of silver would be worth £1.3 million in today's money – a goodly sum. As the millennium arrived, the population of England was about 5 million people, so per capita it was beyond goodly and into crippling. Some of the sums bandied about (and kept deadly secret) in discussions of the late 2017 'Divorce Bill', to separate the UK from the EU, suggest that yet again the British population will find itself crippled. We shall see.

Post-Maldon, the British had imposed on them a Danish king, the famed Cnut (anglice 'Canute'), son of Sweyn Forkbeard and grandson of Harald Bluetooth (the Danes had an enviable forthrightness in naming their high and mighty), paddler in the unlistening ocean.

The following extract is from Rudyard Kipling's poem 'Dane-geld: AD 980–1016' (1911). Its uncompromising message confirms that it should rank high in the Brexit literary florilegium (anthology of literary extracts, forgive my flight of eloquence in the presence of poetry):

It is always a temptation for a rich and lazy nation,
  To puff and look important and to say: –
'Though we know we should defeat you,
  we have not the time to meet you.
  We will therefore pay you cash to go away.'

And that is called paying the Dane-geld;
  But we've proved it again and again,
That if once you have paid him the Dane-geld
  You never get rid of the Dane.

One of the most effective pieces of Leave propaganda, in the run-up to the referendum vote, was a double-decker 'battle bus', with the following inscription on its panels:

WE SEND THE EU £350 MILLION A WEEK!

LET'S FUND OUR NHS INSTEAD

VOTE LEAVE!

LET'S TAKE BACK CONTROL!

It could just as well have carried the message 'No more f*ck*ng Danegeld!'

Domesday Book

Most histories of modern English literature begin their serious business with Geoffrey Chaucer. The good Brexiteer should know and love 'Dan' (Master) Geoffrey, but ignore him. His wonderful poems lie wholly athwart what Brexit stands for.

The poet's name itself – derived from the French *chaussure*, shoemaker (forget, for the moment, the French etymology and pronunciation of 'Farage') – raises a warning flag. It identifies him as being descended from those Norman (that is, French, aboriginally Viking, as we have seen) carpetbaggers who came over with William.[6]

Chaucer's most famous poem, the late fourteenth-century *Canterbury Tales*, chronicles a mixed company making an Easter pilgrimage from London to the shrine of St Thomas à Becket at Canterbury. Thomas, a turbulent priest assassinated by royal command after he overstepped the mark, was also – and more importantly for our purposes – Norman from his mitre to his golden buskins. His father and mother were of Norman heritage. Every strand of DNA and splash of blood on the cathedral floor after the archbishop's infamous murder was Norman. So love Chaucer, laugh till the buttons fly off your weskit at the doings in the 'Miller's Tale', but discard him from the Good Brexiteer's canon.

Recall for a moment the greatest Anglo-Norman of them all, William the Conqueror. There will be more on him and the Norman Yoke thesis (and its modern version, the Brussels Yoke thesis) later. But picture the first thing the conquering William did, Harold having been deoculated by an arrow. William, at his moment of conquest, picked up and swallowed two mouthfuls of Hastings sand. A symbolic act.[7] His mission was thereafter to swallow up the whole of England like so much *rosbif.*

A cunning tyrant with well-thought-out long-term aims, William did not conquer by the sword, but by bureaucracy (a tellingly French word), in the shape of that damnable Domesday Book.[8] It was a veritable Devil's Bible, an instrument (like the European Parliament) of extraterritorial officialdom to raise taxes more efficiently from foreign subjects, our put-upon forefathers.

As the Anglo-Saxon Chronicle records, William, no longer the Conqueror but the Royal Bloodsucker, sent his men all over England into every shire [to] find out how many hides there were in the shire, what land and cattle the king had himself in the shire, what dues he ought to have in twelve months from the shire. Also he had a record made of how much land his archbishops had, his bishops and his abbots and his earls, and what or how much everyone who was in England had ... So very narrowly did he have it investigated that there was no single hide nor yard of land, nor indeed ... one ox or cow or pig which was left out and not put down in his record, and these records were brought to him afterwards.

He evidently valued the porkers in his country more fondly than his biped subjects.

As an example, let us look at Domesday Book's inventory of the aforementioned Maldon (modernized text):

Hundred: Wibrihtesherne
County: Essex
Total population: 54 households
Total tax assessed: 10.2 geld units
Taxable units: Taxable value 5.6 geld units. Taxed
    on 5.58.
Value: Value to lord in 1066: £12. Value to lord in 1086:
    £12. Value to lord c. 1070: £12.
Households: 9 villagers. 10 smallholders. 3 slaves.
Ploughland: 2 lord's plough teams. 5 men's plough
    teams.
Other resources: Meadow 10 acres. Woodland
    50 pigs. 1 mill.
Livestock in 1066: 2 cobs.
Owners: Lord in 1066: Siward (Barn). Lord in 1086:
    Ranulf Peverel.

Those last, note well, are good old English names. Why did Byrhtnoth and his men die, sword in hand, in the mud, if only to pay even more Danegeld in the form of tax to the Norman usurper (the Normans, recall again, are genetically Viking).

Domesday Book is not topography or cartography; it's tax assessment, HMRC in a horned helmet. Those initials, of course, stand for 'Gimme, gimme, gimme.' The Norman Domesday Book prophesies what their successors the EU will do, about a millennium on. Bureaucracy is a one-way ticket to tax, and tax, when levied by a foreign exchequer, is robbery by a nicer name. Who believes the Normans weren't transferring good English pounds back to their European domain, buttering their own pockets en route? The history of England, post-1066, will be a long process of de-Normanizing, and one that goes on – until March 2019, DV.

> MORAL: Their fingers are in your pocket.
> Cut the penny-pickers off.

Postscript: Two Cheers for the Domesday Boke

There are those, of course, who argue that – brutally and by force of arms – William made national sense of the myriad tribal entities that fragmented ancient Britain. French-Norman-Viking that he was, he created the homogeneous entity called England, weaving it from patchwork into the national unity we now have.[9] The Brexiteer (recall Nigel's necktie) will scoff at that, and prefer the most authentic account of William's end, and the recantation he (supposedly) made on his deathbed:

> I treated the native inhabitants of the kingdom with unreasonable severity, cruelly oppressed high and low, unjustly disinherited many, and caused the death of thousands by starvation and war, especially in Yorkshire

... In mad fury I descended on the English of the north like a raging lion, and ordered that their homes and crops with all their equipment and furnishings should be burnt at once and their great flocks and herds of sheep and cattle slaughtered everywhere. So I chaſtised a great multitude of men and women with the lash of ſtarvation and, alas! was the cruel murderer of many thousands, both young and old, of this fair people.

Be warned, England.

The Tattooed Heart

Theresa May went Wittgenstein with the one thing she has said that will, for a certainty, survive her short administration into the library of quotable political quotations: 'Brexit means Brexit.' Boil it down and 'England' is what Brexit 'means' in this tautology.[10] Some of the more passionate Brexiteers declare their faith in what Brexit is about with a tattoo. They'd tattoo 'England' on their heart if they could. Over the heart on the left pectoral has to do, but the thought is there. Cardiac patriotism.[11]

A book no one reads nowadays is Edward Bulwer-Lytton's *Harold: The Last of the Saxon Kings*. A weighty Victorian 'three-decker' (three-volume novel), expatiating (Bulwer-Lytton was a very expatiative writer) on the so-called Norman Yoke thesis, it was published in 1847.

The novel opens in jolly vein: 'Merry was the month of May in the year of our Lord 1052' (a good example of Bulwerese, mercilessly lampooned by Thackeray).[12] England, alas, will be merry no more. Bulwer-Lytton's narrative climaxes with William's invasion, fourteen years later, in the ominous year 1066. A very bad thing.[13]

Bulwer-Lytton creates a wildly fanciful romantic plot round his last Saxon king. Historically, it is well beyond parody, or even Hollywood's treatment of English history.[14] Edith, the ward of Hilda, an ancient Scandinavian prophetess, loves the future King Harold. But he discards her and, for reasons of state, makes a strategic marriage elsewhere. A king must be above mere affairs of the heart, we are to understand (did not Bulwer-Lytton's reigning queen of England, God save her, marry a German princeling?).

After Harold's death in battle at Hastings, Edith roots for his corpse among the slaughtered piles of Saxon nobles, tearing off the dead fighters' armour in her amorous frenzy:

> Her hands bled as the mail gave way to her efforts; the tunic beneath was all dabbled with blood. She rent the folds, and on the breaſt, juſt above the silenced heart, were punctured in the old Saxon letters; the word 'EDITH'; and juſt below, in characters more fresh, the word 'ENGLAND'.

Every great man should have his Edith.

'Where is the Norman now?' Bulwer-Lytton's novel asks in its epilogue. 'Nowhere', is the answer. After 'eight centuries' England has, at last, thrown off the Norman Yoke – only, UKIP would retort, to put it back on again in 1973.

Saxonism, the racial soul of England, reasserted itself in June 2016, after nine centuries. Referenda are quicker than war, and there is less danger of getting an arrow in the eye.[15] Were it a better novel, *Harold: The Last of the Saxon Kings* would be high on the Brexit reading list. One is reluctant, however, to inflict the ten hours it takes to read the narrative on any but card-carrying Victorianists and tattoo artists. But the message is clear enough, and worth reiterating: nothing good comes over the English Channel. Never has, never will.[16] Bulwer-Lytton's novel, popular in its day, popularized in England the Christian names Harold and Edith, and – of course – the cardiac tattoo.

Malory and King Arthur:
The Literary Invention of England

Where does the concept of 'England' originate as something more than geography – 'land of the Angles'? Where is 'England' first articulated as something ideal, something worth dying for, even? Where did it get the heavy ideological baggage it now carries?

Let a famous sonnet, composed in 1914, make clear what one is talking about here – Rupert Brooke's 'The Soldier':

> If I should die, think only this of me:
> That there's some corner of a foreign field
> That is for ever England. There shall be
> In that rich earth a richer dust concealed;
> A dust whom England bore, shaped, made aware,
> Gave, once, her flowers to love, her ways to roam,
> A body of England's, breathing English air,
> Washed by the rivers, blest by suns of home.
>
> And think, this heart, all evil shed away,
> A pulse in the eternal mind, no less
> Gives somewhere back the thoughts by England given;
> Her sights and sounds; dreams happy as her day;
> And laughter, learnt of friends; and gentleness,
> In hearts at peace, under an English heaven.[17]

What is the poet saying? To die for England (the words 'England' and 'English' are six times repeated, 'lest we forget') is a worthwhile thing. Whoever said such a thing about 'Europe'? A *European* heaven? Who would want to spend eternity there?

Brooke wrote his poem after volunteering to die for England, in the First World War. He did indeed die soon afterwards, in transport to action off the coast of Greece, and he is buried on the island of Skyros. An insect bite went septic and killed him.

What, though, is the first great work of literature to articulate the ideal of 'England' that Brooke glorifies in the poem? The question answers itself, for anyone with a passing knowledge of English literary history: the literary idea of 'England' emerges, in its modern form, in a docu-fictional narrative about knights of the realm, and their liege, by a Knight of the Realm – Sir Thomas Malory.

It was Malory who put into print, via his good friend William Caxton, England's first publisher, a work irritatingly miscalled *Le Morte d'Arthur*. Malory called what he wrote *The Whole Book of King Arthur and of his Noble Knights of the Round Table*. The published title was accidentally given by Caxton, who mistook the name of its last section for the name of the whole book; or perhaps, as publishers perennially do, he thought his title would be more eye-catching. As Malory's title implies, in the book – his only work of literature – he set out to retell in English the entire Arthurian story. Ignore Caxton's French title; Malory's text is as English as roast beef and carrots. And both Malory and Caxton (in his editorial preface) are at pains to make clear that the book is about England, and about King Arthur.

Morte d'Arthur has been an inspirational work over the centuries, proliferating, via Spenser's *Faerie Queene* (of which more later), through such rewrites as Tennyson's cobwebby epic *Idylls of the King* (1859–85), T. H. White's *The Once and Future King* (1958), film and the musical *Camelot*.[18] There are computer games that draw on it, as does *Game of Thrones* – big time. The connection between George R. R. Martin and Malory is blogged about indefatigably, but the conscientious Brexiteer should hack his way back and read the Malory original. It's a worthwhile exercise.

Malory's authoritative biographer is P.J.C. Field.[19] It was also Professor Field who wrote a potted life history of the author in the *Dictionary of National Biography*, which I draw on gratefully here.[20]

Malory inherited his station in life, as son and heir of John Malory, Esquire. As Professor Field informs us, with a barrage of medieval cv, Thomas's father was a man of some standing in fifteenth-century England:

> John Malory held the manor of Newbold Revel in Warwickshire, that of Winwick in Northamptonshire, and lands nearby in Leicestershire. He was a person of importance in Warwickshire, where he was sheriff, escheator, justice of the peace, and five times MP, and his brother or cousin Sir Robert Malory was preceptor of the hospitallers of St John of Jerusalem in Warwickshire, and later prior of the hospitallers in England.

One is not sure what all that dignification means ('escheator'?), but it makes the point: Malory senior was 'a person of importance', and a proud member of the gentry – an 'Esquire', though, not an aristocrat.

One of the things one can deduce about Malory junior is that he aimed at a lot more importance than his father bequeathed him. He was prepared to rise in life by crime, if that's what it came to. As it happened, it did, and he turned out to be rather good at it.

Thomas got himself knighted. How is not quite clear, at least not to me. According to some accounts, he may have fought for England against the French, in Gascony. If so, he would certainly have picked up useful fighting skills in that never-ending, Hundred Years War that he would put to personal use later. In 1443, for example, he was accused of robbery with violence near Winwick, Cheshire. He got off and blithely went on to become MP for Warwickshire, and 'a commissioner to assess tax exemptions in the county' – a job in which he, like his successors, could rob without violence. As Don Corleone says, the white-collar crook out-steals the street robber every time.

Malory MP could have lived the life of a well-off country gentleman, as his father had done. But at this point, in 1450, aged about 35, he chose more direct routes to personal advancement using, one assumes, the skills he had picked up slitting French throats. Let Professor Field take up the story at this point:

> With the new decade, however, Malory's life underwent a sudden, startling, and unexplained change. During the first recess of the new parliament, on 4 January 1450, he and twenty-six other armed men allegedly lay in ambush to murder [the Duke of Buckingham] in the abbot's woods at Combe near Newbold Revel [Warwickshire].

There followed a string of flagrant crimes: extortion, theft, rape, cattle rustling, deer stealing and robbery. Most serious was his vandalizing a hunting lodge which Buckingham used. Malory's attack was a deliberate provocation of Buckingham, who was hunting him with a large band of men. Thomas Malory was, nonetheless, returned to the parliament that met in September 1450.

> It was a bad move. In May 1451 York's efforts collapsed, and in July Buckingham caught up with Malory and committed him to the sheriff, who detained him in his own house at Coleshill. Malory escaped by swimming the moat at night, but was recaptured. He was

charged at Nuneaton, the centre of Buckingham's power in Warwickshire, before a court presided over by Buckingham, with a long list of offences including the attempted murder of Buckingham; and when the two juries returned true bills, a writ of *certiorari* transferred the proceedings to the king's bench at Westminster. In January 1452 Malory was in prison in London, awaiting trial. All of this was clearly meant to keep the legal process away from the assize town of Warwick and the influence that Malory's friends might bring to bear there. Someone had also clearly encouraged potential complainants to bring forward every possible charge against him. That does not mean the charges were false.

Malory, to cut a short story even shorter, got off. He was very good at getting off. But his career in low crime continued:

A neighbour's complaint that Malory had stolen her oxen probably dates from this period of freedom, and at the end of it he failed to surrender to his bail; Buckingham had to be called out again to recapture him. Bailed a second time, in 1454, to a group of Norfolk's men, he joined an old crony on a horse-stealing expedition across East Anglia that ended in Colchester gaol. From there he escaped again, 'using swords, daggers, and halberds', but was again recaptured and sent back to London.

Thereafter he was shuttled around various prisons. If you had money, such institutions could be comfortable hostels that just happened to have bars on the windows. Malory had money; but four-star living in prison drained it, and his funds ran out. So, of course, did the comfort. Eventually, in about 1460, he was released by pardons procured by powerful friends in high places.

This most restless of literary rogues could not settle down. He conspired, with others, against the king, Edward IV (we are now in familiar Richard III territory, 'made glorious summer by this sun of York', etc.):

> Malory seems to have been drawn into a plot against [Edward IV] that was discovered in June 1468, and arrested and imprisoned without formal charge, probably in the Tower of London. He was certainly imprisoned in relative comfort and with access to one of the best libraries in the country. This is shown by the *Morte D'Arthur*, which he wrote in prison at this time, and completed by 3 March 1470; but the Yorkists now thought of him as a dangerous enemy, and he was excluded by name from general pardons offered in July 1468 and February 1470.

Malory was freed by amnesty (meaning those friends in high places) in 1471. He was, as Field ironically records,

> buried under a marble tombstone in St Francis's Chapel, Greyfriars, Newgate, which despite its proximity to one of the gaols in which he had been imprisoned, was one of the most fashionable churches in London. His epitaph called him 'valens miles de parochia de Monkenkyrkby' ('valiant knight, of the parish of Monks Kirby').

Sam Peckinpah could have made a great film out of Malory's life – cattle-rustler, bandit, soldier of fortune (let's forget the rape, although Peckinpah might not have). For its star, I'd suggest Jason Statham. I see the bald-pated superhero in my mind's eye now, demonstrating that biceps beat brains every time.

Malory the writer coincided with an all-important moment in English literature: the first English printer, Caxton. The manuscript scriptorium, with six scriveners scraping away, would have taken as long as two years to inscribe a tiny edition of literature as long as Malory's; Caxton's press could 'run off' two hundred in a week. Those figures changed the literary culture of England, and that change would continue for half a millennium, until the web took over, spreading literary content even further afield.[21]

Ranking as England's first bestseller in 1485, *Morte d'Arthur* is still a rollicking good read. Brexiteers ought to lobby to get it put on the National Curriculum. Caxton, who published Chaucer as well as Malory, was a champion of books in the English language – call it King Arthur's language. Arthur was, Caxton said in his introduction to the first edition of *Morte d'Arthur*, the monarch 'most to be remembered among us Englishmen to-fore all other Christian kings' (NB 'us Englishmen').

Malory, the Englishman's Englishman, writes in simple, punchy English. Caxton's *Canterbury Tales* and *Morte d'Arthur* were the two primal works of literature that set English on its long career of becoming supranational, a world language. That is what it is now (to the recent irritation of Germans in the EU, and French members of the EU since forever).[22] Malory's English jumps off the page, as can be seen from the story's opening paragraph:

> It befell in the days of Uther Pendragon, when he was king of all England, and so reigned, that there was a mighty duke in Cornwall that held war against him long time. And the duke was called the Duke of Tintagil. And so by means King Uther sent for this duke, charging him to bring his wife with him, for she was called a fair lady, and a passing wise, and her name was called Igraine.

The duke does as commanded. A 'lusty' monarch, Uther decides on the spot to exercise his *droit de seigneur* on the fair Igraine. The lady proves skittish, however, and she and her husband, a man unwilling to lay down his wife for his king, hie off back to their castle in Cornwall, her virtue unviolated.

His regal rights denied, Uther waxes 'wonderly wroth'. He sends 'plain word' to the duke and threatens that if he doesn't have his way with the fair Igraine, he will come and do to the duke what he does to chickens: 'stuff him' – and roast him on the embers of his burning castle, one may suppose. Unminced words.

When the duke continues to resist, Uther raises an army and marches off to Tintagel. Whether the soldiers knew they were risking their lives so that their leader could get his end away is not recorded. Let Malory take up the tale again at this point:

> Then in all haſte came Uther with a great hoſt, and laid a siege about the caſtle of Terrabil. And there he pight [put up] many pavilions [tents], and there was great war made on both parties, and much people slain. Then for pure anger and for great love of fair Igraine the king Uther fell sick. So came to the king Uther Sir Ulfius, a noble knight, and asked the king why he was sick. I shall tell thee, said the king, I am sick for anger and for love of fair Igraine, that I may not be whole.[23] Well, my lord, said Sir Ulfius, I shall seek Merlin, and he shall do you remedy, that your heart shall be pleased.

Merlin duly helped out, after some rummaging in his magic bag. The duke was slain, fighting to preserve his wife's honour (did Uther arrange that, as David did with Uriah the Hittite?). Before his corpse was cold, Uther was off to Igraine's bedchamber, disguised by Merlin's magic as the duke, back from

victory on the field and rampantly eager for some marital relief.
(A good wife would understand that kind of thing.) The narrative continues:

> after the death of the duke, King Uther lay with Igraine
> more than three hours after his death, and begat on her
> that night Arthur, and on day came Merlin to the king,
> and bade him make him ready, and so he kissed the lady
> Igraine and departed in all haſte.

Thus was England's noblest king 'begat'. A historic sex crime,
as some might see it. Whatever else, it's plainly told.

Such, then, is the birth, not the *morte* (death), of Arthur.
The outline of the Arthurian legend (no one knows if the king
actually existed) needs no description. Everyone knows about
the magical Merlin (inspirer of Hogwarts), the Round Table,
Galahad whose heart was pure, Lancelot whose heart was
impure, Lancelot's paramour Guinevere, the woman who made
adultery stylish, Excalibur, the sword offered in rock for Arthur's
hand only and after Arthur's *morte* returned to the Lady of
the Lake.

The opening sections of Malory's pseudo-chronicle deal
with the adult Arthur's welding England, by force of arms, into
a nation of whom he is first king. The ceremonies of coronation, as described by Malory, closely resemble those of today.
He is never credited. Charles III should tactfully do so, when
he's crowned.

Let's highlight here, however, an episode that is relevant
to current Brexit concerns. Now that it has become, under
Arthur, a national entity, Rome (with the power of the Catholic
Church behind it) sees 'England' as eminently taxable. Call it
Romegeld:

Right so came into the court twelve knights, and were aged men, and they came from the Emperor of Rome, and they asked of Arthur truage [tax] for this realm, other else the emperor would destroy him and his land. Well, said King Arthur, ye are messengers, therefore ye may say what ye will, other else ye should die therefore. But this is mine answer: I owe the emperor no truage, nor none will I hold him, but on a fair field I shall give him my truage that shall be with a sharp spear, or else with a sharp sword, and that shall not be long, by my father's soul, Uther Pendragon. And therewith the messengers departed passingly wroth.

One hears a primeval echo – 'Up yours Delors'.

It is impossible, I think, not to read Malory without feeling that he is closer to us, much closer, than six hundred years.

The Literature of the People

Medieval literature has relatively little articulate political content, and virtually nothing Brexit-flavoured. One salient exception, brief but trenchant, may be called to the Brexiteers' attention. It embodies that surging rebelliousness (up yours!) occasionally voiced in literature. Call it the working-class voice. That voice is a strong element in Brexit discourse, angrily demanding a better society than that in which history has placed us. It has an inchoate energy. One felt that muscle-of-the-people energy driving events on the morning of 24 June 2016.

In the medieval period the most important story was the Bible. Without it, for people of the time, existence was meaningless. But much of the population could not read their own language, let alone the Latin of the standard Bible, imposed on

them by European Rome. The Church and its gowned hiero-
phants monopolized the Bible. Books were hugely expensive
even after the invention of printing in the late fifteenth century.
Those in power have always found an ignorant, illiterate people,
with no power over language (and the dangerous ideas it can
convey), conveniently manageable.[24]

But the people must be fed their stories. The human species
has an appetite for them; indeed, it is one of the things that
make us human. In provincial towns the medieval trade guilds
formed an alliance with the Church and, remotely, Rome, that
far-off European place. The guilds took it upon themselves to
evangelize – spread the good word – by street entertainment,
and drama served that purpose perfectly.

Annually, at some particular holy day in the Christian calen-
dar (our world of packaged 'holiday' still carries the notation),
dramatic 'cycles' – that is, the whole biblical narrative, from
Genesis to Final Judgment – would be staged. Each guild would
sponsor a wagon, or 'float', typically choosing an episode from
the Bible that fitted with their profession. The carpenters, for
example, would tell the story of the Crucifixion (the Cross being
made out of wood); the bargemen might tell the story of Noah
and the Flood.

The established Church was generally tolerant of all this.
Indeed, some clergymen, who would have been far and away
the most literate members of their community, helped to write
the plays, if only to stop them from lapsing into blasphemy
and heresy. The guild stored lavish costumes, props and scripts
for use year after year. Prompt copies have survived for several
of the city-based cycles, notably those of Coventry, Leicester,
York, Chester and Wakefield.

The Mystery plays, as they were called, were immensely
popular in their day – and it was, historically, a fairly long day:
two centuries long. There is no question but that the young

Shakespeare saw them in his childhood Stratford, enjoyed them and was influenced as a dramatist by them. His audience at the Globe theatre would have been as familiar with them as he was.

A particularly fine example of the Mystery genre is the *Second Shepherd's Play* in the Wakefield cycle. It is not a catchy title, but it is great drama. It was probably composed in about 1475, and was performed, with elaborations and topical adaptations, for many decades thereafter annually on the feast of Corpus Christi in May or June.

The Yorkshire town of Wakefield was enriched in the Middle Ages by the wool and leather trades. Sheep and cattle grazed on the grassy hills around the town, which had good communication with the rest of the country and could get its wares to markets in the big cities. Wakefield also had a reputation for particularly enjoying itself at fairs and other public events, and was nicknamed 'Merry Wakefield'. The citizens clearly liked a good laugh, and the *Second Shepherd's Play* supplied annual merriment (it would have been played year in, year out).

The entire Wakefield Mystery cycle encompasses thirty playlets, beginning with the Creation in Genesis and ending with the hanging of Judas in the disciples' gospels. There are, as the title indicates, two shepherds' plays, celebrating the product (wool) that was the source of the town's enviable prosperity.

The second play opens with three shepherds on the Bethlehem hills (manifestly Yorkshire, not Palestine), watching their sheep by night. December is a bitterly cold month to be outdoors tending sheep. The First Shepherd angrily bemoans the English weather and rails against the social oppression, including taxes, that poor folk like themselves must bear while the tax-avoiding rich (Normans, many of them) are snug, well-fed and warm in their beds. (Taxes were imposed by the guilds, as well as by the town authorities: an in-joke.)

Shepherds made the wool that made the wealth that never quite trickled down to them. As the articulate First Shepherd puts it,

> We're so burdened and banned,
> Over-taxed and unmanned,
> We're made tame to the hand
> Of these gentry men.
> Thus they rob us of our rest, may ill-luck them harry!
> These men, they make the plough tarry
> What men say is for the best, we find the contrary, –
> Thus are husbandmen oppressed, in point to miscarry,
> In life,
> Thus hold they us under
> And from comfort sunder.

The enemy is not Rome, but Wakefield's 'gentry men', the bastard thieving elite.

FLASH FORWARD to a case that put a useful puff of wind in the Brexit sails in 2016. Philip Green was an enterprising 'entrepreneur', that word that the French, according to George W. Bush, don't have. Initially making his money in the clothes and fashion business (the 'rag trade'), Green moved on to acquire high-street firms (at one point he aimed at Marks & Spencer) as the route to uber-wealth – billions, not millions. He was also a big, headline-grabbing spender. For one of his birthdays his wife, Tina (his partner in a business as well as a marital sense), bought him a solid gold Monopoly set, with all his acquisitions as metropolitan stops on the board. She was a wife who could afford it, a citizen of Monaco with many of the couple's assets and wealth in her name, allegedly for tax purposes (without proof).

Green's lavishness seemed designed to flaunt itself and attract tabloid attention. As the BBC reported on 14 May 2005,

> British retail billionaire Philip Green has hired chart-topping R&B group Destiny's Child to perform at his son's bar mitzvah.
>
> The stars are set to entertain guests at the three-day event on the French Riviera estimated to have cost the Bhs and Top Shop boss £4m ($7.4m).
>
> Singer Justin Timberlake could also be performing, *The Times* reports.
>
> Mr Green is said to have chartered a plane to fly about 200 of his family's friends to the bash this weekend.
>
> The guests are being put up at the exclusive Hotel du Cap near Cannes, with the actual bar mitzvah itself expected to take place at a synagogue being temporarily set up in the building.
>
> Mr Green, who lives in nearby Monaco, has built up a fortune of more than £3bn.

There were other extravagant junkets. At one, as photographs record, the Greens appeared in Versailles fancy dress – tempting fate, one might think.

Green's business career had been pursued by unsubstantiated allegations of tax evasion and that he sourced some of his high-street fashion products in foreign sweatshops. The Greens did not, of course, reside in suntrap Monaco to sweat.

Green's buccaneering spirit and ability to get things done were liked in high places, and he was knighted in 2006 for services to business and charitable activity. He was now what the First Shepherd in our Mystery play calls a 'gentryman'. He shrugged off newspaper criticism. In August 2010 David Cameron asked him to lead a review of government spending and procurement; spending was, after all, something that Sir Philip knew about.

Green's troubles came with his involvement with British Home Stores, which he had procured ten years previously for £200 million. A venerable eighty-year-old, 180-outlet department store, BHS had once been, but was no more, a market leader. Its day had passed. Glossy high-street rivals did things smarter, and the concept of the 'British home' ('be it ever so humble') was off-puttingly stale in the second millennium. But the firm retained assets in property and its pension fund.[25]

In March 2015, his family enriched by BHS dividends (to the tune of twice what he had paid in 2000, it is estimated, and much of it tax-free thanks to his Monaco-based wife), Green sold the firm to one Dominic Chappell for £1.

The business pages found it an unusual choice. One of the first acts of this three-time bankrupt and failed racing driver with no retail experience was to award himself a salary of £544,000. Over his short ownership, Chappell later confessed to extracting £2.6 million from the firm. Other millions more were allegedly paid out in suspicious consultancy fees.[26]

BHS entered administration on 25 April 2016, eight weeks before the EU referendum, in the biggest high-street crash since Woolworths in 2009. It left a £571 million black hole in the BHS pension fund. If the government's Pension Protection Fund picked up the tab, it would be the taxpayer who would bail out BHS, or what was left of it. The firm's 11,000 employees lost their jobs, and up to 20,000 former employees of BHS faced losing their pensions or having to live on reduced payouts.

Green was resolutely unapologetic: 'If I give you my plane, right?' he snarled at an inquisitive reporter, 'and you tell me you're a great driver and you crash it into the first fucking mountain, is that my fault?'[27] 'Sir Shifty', as he was anointed by the *Daily Mail* and other tabloid newspapers, became the public hate figure of 2016, someone who, it was felt, made incarnate the whole unfairness of things – what the First Shepherd's outburst was all about. Or, if we recall the barrack-room ballad:

> It's the same the whole world over
> Ain't it all a fucking shame.
> It's the rich what gets the pleasure
> It's the poor what gets the blame.

There were moves in Parliament to strip Green of his knighthood, but they came to nothing. He was, one columnist quipped, down to his last two super-yachts, the last in construction during the destruction of BHS at an estimated cost of a cool £100 million. He called the vessel *Lionheart*; it was wittily nicknamed BHS *Destroyer* by the comedian Simon Brodkin.

The Sir Shifty brouhaha reached its abusive climax in the run-up to the referendum. Its effect was diffusive, but materially helpful to the Brexit cause and vote. Who knows, it may even have swung it. It stoked anger among those whom, when he first became prime minister, Tony Blair had called the 'excluded'. The Green publicity died down, to be replaced by other publicity, as 2016 – and its big upset – moved on. But, one can plausibly surmise, it played a part in that upset.

To return to where we started, that sense of angry exclusion is what fuels the First Shepherd's outburst, and that complaint speaks to us with a directness that carries across the centuries and resonates to the present day. 'We can take it' – and have done for centuries: not just in the Second World War, when the slogan was current. But push us too far, you gentry folk, and you'll regret it. Long-stoked resentment, not self-interest, one surmises, was a strong impulse in the Leave vote.

Talk to citizens standing outside any job centre in Wakefield today and I suspect they might well complain in much the same way as did their anonymous sheep-herding predecessor. Certainly with the same rich Yorkshire accent. How did Wakefield vote? Don't ask; the answer's obvious.[28]

The Bloudie Crosse

Edmund Spenser made his start in life by being beastly to the Irish, until a mob of riotous Celts finally rose up, burned his castle and drove the hated Englishman back to where he came from (the Irish would pay for that, when Cromwell came along enforcing a United Kingdom by order of the cannonball). Spenser had determined earlier to make his career as a courtier with a single-minded policy of buttering up his virgin monarch. Hence the first English epic in English, *The Faerie Queene*, an exercise in the higher sycophancy. Each of the poem's six books (twelve were originally planned) celebrates a virtue necessary to a monarchic state – all possessed by the Virgin Queen, we apprehend.

The poem opens ('Book One', virtue 'holiness') with the Red Crosse Knight, in his battered armour,[29] pricking his way across the 'plaine' (England), going nowhere fast, it seems:

But on his breſt *a bloudie Crosse* he bore,
The deare remembrance of his dying Lord,
For whose sweete sake that glorious badge he wore,
And dead as liuing euer him ador'd . . . [my emphasis]

The English flag – the Red Cross's emblem – went on to embellish, doughtily, the UKIP-Brexit address to the English nation in 2016. The 'glorious badge' is prominently brandished by English football fans who would not know Faerie Queene from Fairy washing-up liquid (not that they much like the word 'fairy').[30]

Chargers are out of fashion, other than in the fox hunt and on the polo field, but many a white van still bears the flag proudly. The Labour politician Emily Thornberry injudiciously tweeted a sarcastic comment about a council house with a red-cross flag in the window, and a white van with the same ornament, while doorstepping for the Labour Party. Her disdain cost her dearly at the time. It is not hard to guess how the owner of the van voted. Thornberry has since been more careful in her tweets.

RECALL Bulwer-Lytton's *Harold: The Last of the Saxon Kings* (see 'The Tattooed Heart' above). Tattooists confirm that the Bloudie Cross, routinely combined with 'England' and often accompanied with knightly sword and armour, is a highly popular motif today among a certain class of client. Bicep is nowadays preferred over heart by way of bodily site.

In Sir Walter Scott's great polemic against the Norman Yoke thesis, *Ivanhoe* (more of which later), the hero, Wilfred, is a returned Crusader and, true to his cause, does battle under the banner of the 'Red Cross Knight': just like Spenser's holy hero. So, too, does Nigel Farage, who was photographed in the run-up to the election with a vast red-cross-emblazoned top hat, to go with his Battle of Hastings tie.

The Brexit Boadicea

The *Mail on Sunday* on 9 October 2016 carried the arresting line: 'Theresa May stands like a Brexit Boadicea'.[31] The author of the panegyric was Sir Anthony Seldon, an eminent advocate for independence in every sphere of life, even in the excellent university he leads, which spurns government finance to stand upon its own two feet.[32] May was not merely implementing the will of the people, we were told (loudly). She was doing it in the spirit of one of the most successful army leaders in English military history – and a woman to boot.

Don't put Boadicea's face on a postage stamp. Leave that to Jane Austen, whose achievements were less bloody, bold and resolute. And let Brussels quiver when they contemplate the incarnate spirit of Britain, ancient and modern, in this woman who independently led her people into victorious battle against Imperial Rome in AD 60. 'Theresa May', went Seldon's eulogy,

> ſtands like a Brexit Boadicea, breathing fiery words
> againſt fat cats, gas rip-offs, and her biggeſt bugbear –
> the privileged and the few – as she repositions herself as
> the Tory leader who is the tribune of the working classes.
> It is the moſt opportuniſtic manoeuvre by a woman who
> has quietly risen from a suburban reċtory without trace.

Farewell to the posh chumocracy and all elites when TM/PM is swinging her knockberry. Seldon's article was accompanied by a mash-up photograph of Theresa's head on Boadicea's armoured body, about to bash the brains out of anyone who stood in her way. A red-cross armband had been added to the bicep. Mrs T. had been the iron lady; TM/PM (no feminizing 'Mrs' for Theresa) was steel – silent, gleaming and unbending. Or so everyone thought until 8 June 2017.

The image of Boadicea was very different before she became the bonnet mascot of Brexit and the *Daily Mail*'s icon of feminism militant. The earliest historical accounts pictured the warrior queen of the Iceni tribe as a terrifying virago, a view disseminated by Raphael Holinshed in his sixteenth-century *Chronicles*, that poison well from which Shakespeare sucked up so much bad history:[33]

Hir mightie tall personage, comely shape, severe counte-
nance, and sharpe voyce, with hir long and yealow tresses
of heare reaching downe to hir thighes, hir brave and gorgeous apparell also caused the people to have hir in greate
renounce. She ware a Chaine of golde, greate, and verye
massie, and was clad in a lose kyrtle of sundrie colours,
and aloft thereuppon shee had a thicke Irish mantell:
hereto in his hand (as hir custome was) she bare a speare.

Feminists will note (hackles rising, battleaxes grasped) that even
at that primeval period the stress is not on what Boadicea did or
was, but how she was clad: 'hir brave and gorgeous apparell'. She
might as well have been wearing those £995 gold leather trousers by Amanda Wakeley that handsomely ornamented TM/PM's
pins in publicity photographs in December 2016. Those trousers
provoked ructions ('Trousergate'), which proved that woman
is, in the first analysis, what she wears; man is what he does.
When did anyone say anything about (pussy-grabbing) Donald
Trump's trousers, other than that they seem a little tight round
the seat when the long jackets he protectively wears pull up?

Holinshed based his account on the work of Roman historians, principally Tacitus and Cassius Dio.[34] For them, the
warrior ruler was the enemy of civilization (by which they
meant Imperial Rome), a barbarian, something to be put down.
If she were a woman, that would make two reasons for putting
her down.

The empire's chroniclers, unsurprisingly, did not have all that
warm a feeling for a rebel leader who had impertinently slaughtered ('no prisoners!') as many as 80,000 of their best soldiers
and would in the long run help to drive Rome out of Albion.
They did eventually regain control of their colony, but by then
Boadicea's point had been made: Rome could be shaken, defeated
even. All you needed was unbridled savagery. There followed

150 years of violent relationship before Rome finally gave up on Britannia.

The Iceni, Boadicea's tribe, have left no historical record. What ink (woad) they had, they daubed themselves with before battle. We do not even know their language, other than that it was probably a variant of Celtic. They were a dominant tribe based mainly in what is now East Anglia. There are streets and monuments named after Boadicea in Colchester (my home town), and perhaps a tad of her DNA is present in a few Colcestrian veins, even mine. The idea thrills the blood.

From what we know, the warrior queen of the Iceni had ample reason for her rebellion, and for the ruthlessness of her acts as leader. Her husband, the elderly King Prasutagus, had made an uneasy pact with Rome. He accepted foreign rule and paid the demanded tribute (the Iceni were good at making coins, one of the more interesting aspects that archaeology has recently discovered about them).

On his death, Prasutagus' will left half his kingdom to the far-off, wanton Emperor Nero, as an act of fidelity. The other half was left to the king's young daughters, to maintain his bloodline; Boadicea would presumably act as vicegerent until the young women grew up. Prasutagus, Tacitus records, had amassed considerable wealth (hence the surviving coinage).

Nero was not a giving emperor, however. He wanted the lot. Boadicea's legal appeals were ignored, and in the face of her stubbornness the emperor resolved to make an example. Such things were routine in AD 61. She was publicly flogged in front of her people, a punishment usually reserved for slaves, and designed to humiliate her. And it hurt: the whip was reportedly of leather knotted and loaded with metal, to cut deeper into the flesh.

Boadicea's daughters (twelve years old, it is recorded by Tacitus) were publicly gang-raped by soldiery, in front of their mother's eyes. It was theatre of cruelty punishment, which usually worked for Rome, but it had an opposite effect on the Iceni. Fired by personal indignation, Boadicea raised a revolt. Cassius Dio tells us that she consulted the Celtic war goddess, Andraste, before loosing her dogs of war – literally:

> 'Let us, therefore, go againſt [the Romans], truſting boldly to good fortune. Let us show them that they are hares and foxes trying to rule over dogs and wolves.' When she [Boadicea] had finished speaking, she employed a species of divination, letting a hare escape from the fold of her dress; and since it ran on what they considered the auspicious side, the whole multitude shouted with pleasure, and Boudica, raising her hand toward heaven, said: 'I thank you, Andraſte, and call upon you as woman speaking to woman . . . I beg you for victory and preservation of liberty.'

This may not be historically reliable testimony, but there is something glorious about it. 'Woman speaking to woman' has a modern ring to it.

More to the point, the Iceni's light, wicker-armoured chariots, the tribe's knowledge of the thickly forested terrain and their skills in skirmish and surprise attack were a crucial feature of her campaign, which Boadicea led personally from the front. The Roman commander, Suetonius, was distracted by a simultaneous uprising in Wales, and his anti-Iceni forces were depleted. Initially Boadicea gained the upper hand. She conquered, sacked, looted and terrorized the major Roman towns around East Anglia. Her unleashed brutality as barbarian victrix went beyond even that of Rome, but this was a strategic mistake that would cost her dear. According to Graham Webster, author of the standard biography,

The Iceni took the heads of their captives and offered them to the goddess of victory, as this was customary of the Celts. However, while storming the city of London, Dio Cassius gives a detailed description of the torturing of the Roman women: 'their breasts were cut off and stuffed in their mouths, so that they seemed to be eating them, then their bodies were skewered lengthwise on sharp stakes'.[35]

The result of this bloody uprising, unsurprisingly, was to make the Romans, when they counter-attacked, seem like saviours from this harpy queen. Suetonius' reinforced regiments eventually won in a battle on open ground, where military tactics were decisive, and order was restored. But for 150 years, until Rome eventually went back home, it was always a fraying order. Pax Romana never really took root in Britannia.

A LOW OPINION of Boadicea was one of the Romans' long-lasting legacies. John Milton, a Latinist to the core, called her a 'distracted woeman, with as mad a crew at her heels' ('woeman' is a pun on 'woman' and 'woe' – Milton had a lot of woe with the women in his life. So, of course, did Adam in *Paradise Lost*).

The image of the warrior queen was rehabilitated by the excessively English poet William Cowper in his poem 'Boadicea: An Ode' (1782). A druid prophet is pictured, urging a bleeding, violated Boadicea into battle not for her injured self, or her tribe, or for her daughters, but for her nation:

> Rome shall perish – write that word
>   In the blood that she has spilt;
> Perish hopeless and abhorr'd,
>   Deep in ruin as in guilt.

Rome for empire far renown'd,
Tramples on a thousand ſtates,
Soon her pride shall kiss the ground –
Hark! the Gaul is at her gates.[36]

A thousand states? Change that to 28 vassal states.

Boadicean glorification peaked during the Victorian period. The warrior queen's name, those without a ready command of the Iceni tongue were informed, literally means 'Victory'. The reigning queen, Victoria, was baptized a 'namesake'. Her faithful poet laureate, Alfred, Lord Tennyson, was inspired (nudged, perhaps) to write a poem, 'Boadicea', a panegyric. Those for whom such things matter will appreciate that Tennyson wrote it in the fiendishly difficult galliambic metre. Perhaps because of this literary feat, it was one of the poet's own favourite works:

While about the shore of Mona those Neronian
   legionaries
Burnt and broke the grove and altar of the Druid and
   Druidess,
Far in the Eaſt Boadicea, ſtanding loftily charioted,
Mad and maddening all that heard her in her fierce
   volubility,
Girt by half the tribes of Britain, near the colony
   Camulodune,[37]
Yell'd and shriek'd between her daughters o'er a wild
   confederacy.
'They that scorn the tribes and call us Britain's
   barbarous populaces,
Did they hear me, would they liſten, did they pity me
   supplicating?
Shall I heed them in their anguish? shall I brook to
   be supplicated?

Hear Icenian, Catieuchlanian, hear Coritanian,
    Trinobant!
Muſt their ever-ravening eagle's beak and talon
    annihilate us?
Tear the noble heart of Britain, leave it gorily
    quivering?
Bark an answer, Britain's raven! bark and blacken
    innumerable,
Blacken round the Roman carrion, make the carcase
    a skeleton,
Kite and keſtrel, wolf and wolfkin, from the
    wilderness, wallow in it,
Till the face of Bel be brighten'd, Taranis be
    propitiated.
Lo their colony half-defended! lo their colony,
    Camulodune!
There the horde of Roman robbers mock at a
    barbarous adversary.
There the hive of Roman liars worship a gluttonous
    emperor-idiot.
Such is Rome, and this her deity: hear it, Spirit of
    Cassivelaun!'

This, surely, is a poem that the Brexiteer should clutch to their heart, although Bel and Taranis are a bit puzzling.

Boadicea in Stone

As part of the Victorian glorification of Boadicea, an equestrian statue of the Iceni queen was commissioned in the 1850s from the eminent sculptor Thomas Thornycroft, who had done a fine bronze of Queen Victoria, horsed, for the Great

Exhibition of 1851. Prince Albert took a great interest in the Boadicea project, but died in 1861, before it got under way. Funding for the bronze was slow coming. Nonetheless Thornycroft had a full model made before his death, in 1885. It was not yet clear where would be the best site.

Thirteen years later sufficient funds were available, and the statue finally came into being in 1902, at Westminster Pier, opposite what is now grandly called Portcullis House (evoking another period of English history), where MPS have offices, chambers and luncheon facilities (heavily subsidized at taxpayers' expense. Whenever I lunch there I remark that I'm paying for the meal twice. My friends are getting rather tired of the jest).

Thornycroft's large sculpture shows the warrior queen in her chariot, two undraped-to-the-waist daughters behind her, charging towards Big Ben, not waiting, one guesses, for the little green man. Her intention, presumably, is to do to the English Parliament what she had done to Londinium two millennia previously. The inscription on the noble erection reads:

BOADICEA
(BOUDICCA)
QUEEN OF THE ICENI
WHO DIED A.D. 61
AFTER LEADING HER PEOPLE
AGAINST THE ROMAN INVADER

Cowper's ode is inscribed on the right-hand side of the plinth. It's a pity one can't read it because of the surrounding stalls selling tawdry (but British!) souvenirs. Bobbies' hats are particularly popular.

Enter the Maybot,
Clanking

After the awful night of 8 June 2017, Theresa May was, as the developers say, 'reimagined' in her nation's mind. She was no longer Boadicea rediviva. That image was gone forever. *The Guardian*'s political sketch writer, John Crace, had jested many times at the peculiarly mechanical quality of TM/PM's demeanour and public speaking, and now he reimagined her as the 'Maybot'. Despite Isaac Asimov's predictions about the future robot-run world, TM/PM was not a very useful bot. She had clangingly led her party from narrow, but workable, majority to ramshackle minority government sustained by a 'bung' to Irish Unionists. The mess she had created seemed to have escaped the TM/PM's notice.

This is how Crace portrayed the cyborg PM the morning after, on 9 June 2017:

> After a morning's work of emergency repairs to her circuits, which had overloaded the night before, the Maybot was eventually in a fit state to meet the Queen shortly after 12 o'clock. Her husband Philip put her through her final tests. 'Who are you?' he asked.
>
> 'I am the Supreme Leader,' the Maybot replied, rather more confidently than she felt.
>
> 'What do you want?'
>
> 'Strong and stable. Strong and stable'.
>
> There were still a few software adjustments to be made but they would have to wait, as the car had already been parked outside the front door of No 10 for more than 20 minutes.

There is, I always think, just the hint of Terminator 2017 in the Craceian Maybot.

Crace ran joyously with his Maybot invention. The image stuck, despite May's protest 'I am not a robot.' It passed the ultimate sales test: it was stolen. The Maybot caricature influenced the nation's reduced and increasingly contemptuous estimate of TM/PM. Satire works if it's done well, and none did it better in 2017 than Crace of *The Guardian*.

There were one or two fitful efforts, as the Maybot clanked her way forward, to redefine TM/PM as a political zombie, but they didn't really come off. The woman who had coined the sentence that would have baffled Wittgenstein, 'Brexit means Brexit', was, and always will be, the Maybot – until, that is, she is TM again, minus the PM.

Fee-Fi-Fo-Fum: I Smell the Blood of an Englishman!

The fact is not prominent in the author profile on the back flap of this book that I am a 'Junior Leader'. What that means is that I have been trained to discuss narrative – children's stories – with children. Kinderseminars.

The stories are still around as they have been for centuries. They perennially fascinate kids (which is why we use them at bedtime). They bear witness to love of narrative and the truths it contains, as a distinctive feature of our species from childhood to death: *Homo narrativus*.

Children's stories are relatively little examined by literary critics, but they bear study, not least because they have some strange aspects. Why, one might ask, do they contain so much violence and nastiness; why are stepmothers so rotten and siblings (think of Cinderella) so mean – until, that is, Prince

Charming comes along?[38] Why does he have to be a prince? Ask the former Ms Middleton.

Obvious answers suggest themselves to Freudianists. Snow White's middle-aged stepmother hates her post-pubescent stepdaughter because she, now, is the 'fairest of them all'. Ma can't turn the clock back, so she'll murder her daughter instead. That will work. The mirror will say the right thing then.

There is nonetheless much that remains provocatively elusive in the classic fairy story. The first lesson Junior Leaders like me must learn is not to tell children what you know. Throw out for discussion what you don't know, what you're not sure about. What has always perplexed you about this or that story or rhyme? For example, in 'Little Red Riding Hood' (still, I think, a firm favourite at bedtime), what is the heroine's grandmother doing living by herself in a remote part of a wolf-infested forest? This is social care, Brothers Grimm-style? Why is the little heroine wearing a 'riding hood', when she walks everywhere?

If we switch to the nursery rhyme 'Jack and Jill':

> Jack and Jill went up the hill
> To fetch a pail of water.
> Jack fell down and broke his crown,
> And Jill came tumbling after.

Why go *up* a hill to get a pail of water? Infants are by and large not au fait with hydrodynamics, but they surely know that more water is to be found at the bottom of hills.

Now we move on to my favourite children's story, 'Jack and the Beanstalk', and its near neighbour 'Jack the Giant Killer'. They are, I suggest, suggestive bedtime reading for every little Brexiteer. The origins of these two 'Jack' tales have been traced back to well before the Middle Ages. They are primeval stories whose origins pre-date 'English literature' in manuscript, print and internet by as much as 5,000 years, it has been calculated.[39]

It was the seventeenth-century French translator and modernizer Charles Perrault, a man of the European Enlightenment, who popularized the traditional children's story – and, in a sense, standardized them for centuries afterwards. The oral became the printed. Before print every village, and within it every family, would have their different versions of children's tales and rhymes, many of them brutal (in the primeval 'Snow White', for example, the princess is violated in her sleep). But unlike, say, Bluebeard, 'Barbe Bleue' (the career wife-killer), the 'Jack' fables are English to the core. 'Jack' is an archetypally English forename, hence, for example, 'Union Jack', 'Jack Tar', 'Jack of all trades', 'Jack be nimble', 'Jack the Ripper', 'Jack and Jill', 'Jumpin' Jack Flash'. And, of course, 'Jack and the Beanstalk'.

You'll remember how the last tale goes, from bedtimes years ago. What follows is my personal favourite of the Victorian printed versions, that by Joseph Jacobs in 1890. It does not, as twentieth-century versions tend to, cut out the bloodier, cannibalistic aspects. Jacobs claimed he had first heard it, thirty years previously, in Australia:

> There was once upon a time a poor widow who had an only son named Jack, and a cow named Milky-White. And all they had to live on was the milk the cow gave every morning, which they carried to the market and sold. But one morning Milky-White gave no milk, and they didn't know what to do.
>
> 'What shall we do, what shall we do?' said the widow, wringing her hands.
>
> 'Cheer up, mother, I'll go and get work somewhere,' said Jack.

'We've tried that before, and nobody would take you,' said his mother. 'We must sell Milky-White and with the money start a shop, or something.'

'All right, mother,' says Jack. 'It's market day today, and I'll soon sell Milky-White, and then we'll see what we can do.'

So he took the cow's halter in his hand, and off he started. He hadn't gone far when he met a funny-looking old man, who said to him, 'Good morning, Jack.'

'Good morning to you,' said Jack, and wondered how he knew his name.

'Well, Jack, and where are you off to?' said the man.

'I'm going to market to sell our cow there.'

'Oh, you look the proper sort of chap to sell cows,' said the man. 'I wonder if you know how many beans make five.'

'Two in each hand and one in your mouth,' says Jack, as sharp as a needle.

'Right you are,' says the man, 'and here they are, the very beans themselves,' he went on, pulling out of his pocket a number of strange-looking beans. 'As you are so sharp,' says he, 'I don't mind doing a swap with you – your cow for these beans.'

'Go along,' says Jack. 'Wouldn't you like it?'

'Ah! You don't know what these beans are,' said the man. 'If you plant them overnight, by morning they grow right up to the sky.'

'Really?' said Jack. 'You don't say so.'

'Yes, that is so. And if it doesn't turn out to be true you can have your cow back.'

'Right,' says Jack, and hands him over Milky-White's halter and pockets the beans.

Back goes Jack home, and as he hadn't gone very far it wasn't dusk by the time he got to his door.

'Back already, Jack?' said his mother. 'I see you haven't got Milky-White, so you've sold her. How much did you get for her?'

'You'll never guess, mother,' says Jack.

'No, you don't say so. Good boy! Five pounds? Ten? Fifteen? No, it can't be twenty.'

'I told you you couldn't guess. What do you say to these beans? They're magical. Plant them overnight and –'

'What!' says Jack's mother. 'Have you been such a fool, such a dolt, such an idiot, as to give away my Milky-White, the best milker in the parish, and prime beef to boot, for a set of paltry beans? Take that! Take that! Take that! And as for your precious beans here they go out of the window. And now off with you to bed. Not a sup shall you drink, and not a bit shall you swallow this very night.'

So Jack went upstairs to his little room in the attic, and sad and sorry he was, to be sure, as much for his mother's sake as for the loss of his supper.

At last he dropped off to sleep.

When he woke up, the room looked so funny. The sun was shining into part of it, and yet all the rest was quite dark and shady. So Jack jumped up and dressed himself and went to the window. And what do you think he saw? Why, the beans his mother had thrown out of the window into the garden had sprung up into a big beanstalk that went up and up and up till it reached the sky. So the man spoke truth after all.

The beanstalk grew up quite close past Jack's window, so all he had to do was to open it and give a jump on to the beanstalk that ran up just like a big ladder. So Jack climbed, and he climbed, and he climbed, and he climbed, and he climbed, and he climbed, and he climbed till at last he reached the sky. And when he got there he found a long broad road going as straight as a dart. So he walked along, and he walked along, and he walked along till he came to a great big tall house, and on the doorstep there was a great big tall woman.

'Good morning, mum,' says Jack, quite polite-like. 'Could you be so kind as to give me some breakfast?' For he hadn't had anything to eat, you know, the night before, and was as hungry as a hunter.

'It's breakfast you want, is it?' says the great big tall woman. 'It's breakfast you'll be if you don't move off from here. My man is an ogre and there's nothing he likes better than boys broiled on toast. You'd better be moving on or he'll be coming.'

'Oh! please, mum, do give me something to eat, mum. I've had nothing to eat since yesterday morning, really and truly, mum,' says Jack. 'I may as well be broiled as die of hunger.'

Well, the ogre's wife was not half so bad after all. So she took Jack into the kitchen, and gave him a hunk of bread and cheese and a jug of milk. But Jack hadn't half finished these when *thump! thump! thump!* the whole house began to tremble with the noise of some-one coming.

'Goodness gracious me! It's my old man,' said the ogre's wife. 'What on earth shall I do? Come along quick and jump in here.' And she bundled Jack into the oven just as the ogre came in.

He was a big one, to be sure. At his belt he had three calves strung up by the heels, and he unhooked them and threw them down on the table and said, 'Here, wife, broil me a couple of these for breakfast. Ah! What's this I smell?

Fee-fi-fo-fum,

I smell the blood of an Englishman,

Be he alive, or be he dead,

I'll have his bones to grind my bread.'

'Nonsense, dear,' said his wife. 'You're dreaming. Or perhaps you smell the scraps of that little boy you liked so much for yesterday's dinner. Here, you go and have a wash and tidy up, and by the time you come back your breakfast'll be ready for you.'

So off the ogre went, and Jack was just going to jump out of the oven and run away when the woman told him not. 'Wait till he's asleep,' says she; 'he always has a doze after breakfast.'

Well, the ogre had his breakfast, and after that he goes to a big chest and takes out a couple of bags of gold, and down he sits and counts till at last his head began to nod and he began to snore till the whole house shook again.

Then Jack crept out on tiptoe from his oven, and as he was passing the ogre, he took one of the bags of gold under his arm, and off he pelters till he came to the beanstalk, and then he threw down the bag of gold, which, of course, fell into his mother's garden, and then he climbed down and climbed down till at last he got home and told his mother and showed her the gold and said, 'Well, mother, wasn't I right about the beans? They are really magical, you see.'

So they lived on the bag of gold for some time, but at last they came to the end of it, and Jack made up his mind to try his luck once more at the top of the beanstalk. So one fine morning he rose up early, and got on to the beanstalk, and he climbed, and he climbed, and he climbed, and he climbed, and he climbed, and he climbed till at last he came out on to the road again and up to the great tall house he had been to before. There, sure enough, was the great tall woman a-standing on the doorstep.

'Good morning, mum,' says Jack, as bold as brass, 'could you be so good as to give me something to eat?'

'Go away, my boy,' said the big tall woman, 'or else my man will eat you up for breakfast. But aren't you the youngster who came here once before? Do you know, that very day my man missed one of his bags of gold.'

'That's strange, mum,' said Jack, 'I dare say I could tell you something about that, but I'm so hungry I can't speak till I've had something to eat.'

Well, the big tall woman was so curious that she took him in and gave him something to eat. But he had scarcely begun munching it as slowly as he could when *thump! thump!* they heard the giant's footstep, and his wife hid Jack away in the oven.

All happened as it did before. In came the ogre as he did before, said, 'Fee-fi-fo-fum,' and had his breakfast off three broiled oxen.

Then he said, 'Wife, bring me the hen that lays the golden eggs.' So she brought it, and the ogre said, 'Lay,' and it laid an egg all of gold. And then the ogre began to nod his head, and to snore till the house shook.

Then Jack crept out of the oven on tiptoe and caught hold of the golden hen, and was off before you could say 'Jack Robinson'. But this time the hen gave a cackle that woke the ogre, and just as Jack got out of the house he heard him calling, 'Wife, wife, what have you done with my golden hen?'

And the wife said, 'Why, my dear?'

But that was all Jack heard, for he rushed off to the beanstalk and climbed down like a house on fire. And when he got home he showed his mother the wonderful hen, and said 'Lay' to it; and it laid a golden egg every time he said 'Lay.'

Well, Jack was not content, and it wasn't long before he determined to have another try at his luck up there at the top of the beanstalk. So one fine morning, he rose up early and got to the beanstalk, and he climbed, and he climbed, and he climbed, and he climbed till he got to the top. But this time he knew better than to go straight to the ogre's house. And when he got near it, he waited behind a bush till he saw the ogre's wife come out with a pail to get some water, and then he crept into the house and got into the copper. He hadn't been there long when he heard *thump! thump! thump!* as before, and in came the ogre and his wife.

'Fee-fi-fo-fum, I smell the blood of an Englishman,' cried out the ogre. 'I smell him, wife, I smell him.'

'Do you, my dearie?' says the ogre's wife. 'Then, if it's that little rogue that stole your gold and the hen that laid the golden eggs he's sure to have got into the oven.' And they both rushed to the oven. But Jack wasn't there, luckily, and the ogre's wife said, 'There you are again with your fee-fi-fo-fum. Why, of course, it's the boy you caught last night that I've just broiled for your breakfast. How forgetful I am, and how careless you are not to know the difference between live and dead after all these years.'

So the ogre sat down to the breakfast and ate it, but every now and then he would mutter, 'Well, I could have sworn –' and he'd get up and search the larder and the cupboards and everything, only, luckily, he didn't think of the copper.

After breakfast was over, the ogre called out, 'Wife, wife, bring me my golden harp.' So she brought it and put it on the table before him. Then he said, 'Sing!' and the golden harp sang most beautifully. And it went on singing till the ogre fell asleep, and commenced to snore like thunder.

Then Jack lifted up the copper-lid very quietly and got down like a mouse and crept on hands and knees till he came to the table, when up he crawled, caught hold of the golden harp and dashed with it towards the door. But the harp called out quite loud, 'Master! Master!' and the ogre woke up just in time to see Jack running off with his harp.

Jack ran as fast as he could, and the ogre came rushing after, and would soon have caught him, only Jack had a start and dodged him a bit and knew where he was going. When he got to the beanstalk the ogre was not more than twenty yards away when suddenly he saw Jack disappear like, and when he came to the end of the road he saw Jack underneath climbing down for dear life. Well, the ogre didn't like trusting himself to such a ladder, and he stood and waited, so Jack got another start. But just then the harp cried out, 'Master! Master!' and the ogre swung himself down on to the beanstalk, which shook with his weight. Down climbs Jack, and after him climbed the ogre. By this time Jack had climbed down and climbed down and climbed down till he was very nearly home. So he called out, 'Mother! Mother! Bring me an axe, bring me an axe.' And his mother came rushing out with the axe in her hand, but when she came to the beanstalk she stood stock still with fright, for there she saw the ogre with his legs just through the clouds.

But Jack jumped down and got hold of the axe and gave a chop at the beanstalk, which cut it half in two. The ogre felt the beanstalk shake and quiver, so he stopped to see what was the matter. Then Jack gave another chop with the axe, and the beanstalk was cut in two and began to topple over. Then the ogre fell down and broke his crown, and the beanstalk came toppling after.

Then Jack showed his mother his golden harp, and what with showing that and selling the golden eggs, Jack and his mother became very rich, and he married a great princess, and they lived happy ever after.

Here are the questions I, as a Junior Leader, would ask:

1   How does the strange old man know Jack's name?
2   Why is there no mention in the tale of Jack's father? Is the 'Giant' or 'Ogre' somehow a father?
3   Where has the Giant been all night?
4   Why does Jack go up the beanstalk a third time?
5   What is the significance of the beans? (Adult male readers will think of erection and wet dreams.)

And a question for the Brexiteer: why is the giant so angry with 'Englishmen'?

It is worth noting that young Will Shakespeare seems to have had 'Jack and the Beanstalk' and 'Jack the Giant Killer' read to him at his bedtime in Stratford. When, in *King Lear*, Edgar comes on the heath, pretending to be poor mad Tom, among his ravings is 'Fie, foh, and fum,/ I smell the blood of a British man.'[40] One catches a glimpse of a little boy in Stratford, listening to his mother, as the candle burns down to the saucer, and thinking.

Shakespeare: 'This England'

Every knowledgeable Brexiteer will be up with Shakespeare, who was voted the Greatest Ever Englishman in BBC Radio 4's *Today* programme poll in 1999, as the millennium turned. Among Shakespeare's anthems to the country that so esteems him, the following protestation will be at home in every Brexiteer's mouth:

> This England never did, nor never shall,
> Lie at the proud foot of a conqueror,
> But when it first did help to wound itself.
> Now these her princes are come home again,
> Come the three corners of the world in arms,
> And we shall shock them. Nought shall make us rue,
> If England to itself do rest but true.

It's well known and much repeated (particularly the last line), but recalling, from the top of the head, where this speech is to be found in the 39-strong Shakespearian corpus may flummox a bit. It, and who utters it, would make a worthy *University Challenge* question; fingers would hover uncertainly over buzzers.

The above are the last lines (signalled by the jingling cumulative couplet) in *King John* – 'not a good man' (as A. A. Milne's doggerel reminds us):

> King John was not a good man –
> He had his little ways.
> And sometimes no one spoke to him
> For days and days and days.

Shakespeare does not at all contradict this nursery-rhyme judgement in his characterization of the monarch. But the play has interesting Brexit-relevant aspects. *King John* is a history play whose history is centred on the subject of English independence from Europe. It opens with France's emissaries making outrageous demands of the English king, with threats of war if Europe's exactions are not heeded. Then comes Rome with yet more exactions. The old story, one might think, going right back to muddy Byrhtnoth.

The terminal Anglophile lines are spoken by the most heroic – and patriotic – character in the play: Sir Philip the Bastard. His is not, on the face of it, a happy title, nor one that indicates a high position in the English line of precedence. Normally, one recalls, the last lines of a Shakespeare play are given to the senior surviving personage (here the son of King John and heir apparent, Prince Henry, who it is hoped will be a better man than his father). That convention symbolizes the return of hierarchy, proper succession (no bastards, see Edmund's end in *Lear*) and good order after whatever turmoil the drama may have depicted. But in this play the new England, we infer, will be created by those outside the existing institutions of state – even the institution of marriage, which guarantees lineage.

The 'Bastard' in *King John* is the illegitimate son of Richard the Lionheart, a very good man. It is implied throughout the play that Philip would be the best ruler England could have in the present dire circumstances – tyrannical as his crowning would have to be. Nothing, however, is stable in *King John*. The play leaves England with a Damoclean sword over its head, still under threat of foreign domination. The last line's stressed word 'If' rings in the ear. Will England rest true?[41]

King John is not a play that is often revived, even in the reconstructed Globe theatre. But it is one, I suggest, that is peculiarly appropriate to our time, and, most centrally, to the crucial years

2016–22. The sword hovers over us yet again. Will England, during these interminable negotiations (I write this parenthesis in June 2018), 'rest true'? It's a big 'If'.

One can digress for a moment to ponder another of Shakespeare's great works relevant to the breaking away (breaking free) of England from Europe. *Cymbeline* is, like *King John*, one of the less performed and read of his works. But, also like *King John*, it is peculiarly relevant to where the country is in the second and third decades of the twenty-first century.

The action is set back into Roman England, time and place mythically hazed. The great political issue opens in Cymbeline's court with him refusing to pay the demanded 'British tribute' (our old friend Danegeld) to Rome, which 'owns' Britain but, mysteriously, seems to have no troops garrisoned there. Cymbeline is warned by the emperor's ambassador that refusal to pay the tribute means invasion and the dogs of war, which are duly let loose. Things in the interim get very complicated, but the big question hovers: will Cymbeline bow the knee to Europe or fight for his country's independence from it?

The play starts many hares. For one thing, Britain too is an imperial power, doing to Wales what Rome is doing to England. There is no devolution yet, and probably never will be. Astonishingly, it all ends with appeasement. Cymbeline, having vanquished the Roman army in battle and taken its chiefs hostage, nonetheless pays up, out of pacifist motives:

> My peace we will begin. And, Caius Lucius,
> Although the victor, we submit to Caesar,
> And to the Roman empire; promising
> To pay our wonted tribute . . .

Is Cymbeline a 'Remoaner'? This is a problem play, and in this genre Shakespeare never offers facile solutions.

Shakespeare's most famous eulogy for England needs no context. It is, of course, the dying John of Gaunt's speech in *Richard II*. Deathbed declaration has a peculiar legal force, and Gaunt (by name and now in body) lays out his Edenic vision of England, God's country, and his tutelage of England's serving (but not for long) monarch:

> This royal throne of kings, this scepter'd isle,
> This earth of majesty, this seat of Mars,
> This other Eden, demi-paradise,
> This fortress built by Nature for herself
> Against infection and the hand of war,
> This happy breed of men, this little world,
> This precious stone set in the silver sea,
> Which serves it in the office of a wall,
> Or as a moat defensive to a house,
> Against the envy of less happier lands,
> This blessed plot, this earth, this realm, this England

England, the pedantic may well object, is not an island. Nor (as the hired assistance of outflung Ulster and the DUP by TM/PM reminds us) is the United Kingdom. But it would be hard to find a more glorious anticipation of what England/the UK stands for over the centuries. Until, that is, 300,000 'aliens' a year started arriving. Its 'happy breed of men', Gaunt stresses, must, above all, not be sullied by European miscegenation.

But, as the eloquent Fintan O'Toole pointed out in an irritatedly corrective article in the *Irish Times* (1 July 2016), in the immediate aftermath of Brexit's triumph, Shakespeare's history was as shaky as his geography:

> John of Gaunt was Jean of Ghent, as in the city that is now part of Belgium. He was a French-speaking

Plantaganet who spent much of his time in Aquitaine and became, for 15 years, titular king of Castile. When the actual people of England rose up in the peasants' revolt of 1381, John of Gaunt was at the top of their hit list.

A Belgian! What right does he, of all people, have to eulogize England? O'Toole continues:

> In any case, if you read the full speech it is not at all the hymn to English perfection suggested by its most famous lines ... The purpose of Gaunt's hyperbole is to point up a contrast between this imaginary England and the actual place as it is under Richard's reign: broke and mortgaged to the hilt. The imaginary island 'bound with the triumphant sea' is in reality 'bound in with shame', awash with 'rotten parchment bonds'. The speech is not a panegyric on England but a complaint about the country being in hock to bondholders.

O'Toole makes a telling point, and it raises a tantalizing question. How would England's greatest Englishman have voted on 23 June 2016?

The nation's relationship with Shakespeare has undergone other alterations in this all-change contemporary period. Most dramatic was the rehabilitation of the great villain king, the man under the black crown, the deformed – in every sense – Richard III. The king's remains, DNA confirmed, were found, ignominiously but wonderfully (spiritual vibration from an astral plane seems to have come into it), in a Leicester city car park ('a Ford, a Ford, my kingdom for a Ford! Or, failing that, a Punto will do'). Various corrections of legend, much of it propagated by Shakespeare and behind him Holinshed, followed. The skeleton testified that Richard was not physically monstrous. He may even, perish the thought, have been a good monarch, despite the millions he now owed in parking fees.[42]

For my money, the finest pro-Brexit words to be found in the Shakespearian corpus come from Richard's mouth. He delivers a wonderfully sneering speech to his army, raring to repel the invader, about the frog army who have dared to breach the borders of the aforesaid scepter'd isle, against every Yorkist visa requirement:

> What shall I say more than I have inferr'd?
> Remember whom you are to cope withal;
> A sort of vagabonds, rascals, and runaways,
> A scum of Bretons, and base lackey peasants,
> Whom their o'er-cloyed country vomits forth
> To desperate ventures and assured destruction.
> You sleeping safe, they bring to you unrest;
> You having lands, and blest with beauteous wives,
> They would restrain the one, distain the other.
> And who doth lead them but a paltry fellow,
> Long kept in Bretagne at our mother's cost?
> A milk-sop, one that never in his life
> Felt so much cold as over shoes in snow?
> Let's whip these stragglers o'er the seas again;
> Lash hence these overweening rags of France,
> These famish'd beggars, weary of their lives;
> Who, but for dreaming on this fond exploit,
> For want of means, poor rats, had hang'd themselves:
> If we be conquer'd, let men conquer us,
> And not these bastard Bretons; whom our fathers
> Have in their own land beaten, bobb'd, and thump'd,
> And in record, left them the heirs of shame.
> Shall these enjoy our lands? lie with our wives?
> Ravish our daughters?

Farage (despite his embarrassingly French name) couldn't have said it better. Richard loses, of course, and goes for his long rest in the Leicester car park. But UKIP, as I said, hallows 'glorious losers'. Richard III, along with Byrhtnoth (both of whom died in good English mud), tops that list.

The Oxford Book of English Verse

If the Brexiteer has just the one book of verse on their shelf, it should be *The Oxford Book of English Verse* (OBEV), specifically the edition that was compiled in 1900. The compiler was 'Q' – Arthur Quiller-Couch – a scholar professor who is now forgotten but who was culturally dominant in his day. It was a day, at the end of Victoria's reign, when England was still confident about its imperial self, and proud of its prideful verse.

If there is one thing England is foremost in, it is not making cars (leave that to the Germans) but turning out verse on its world-beating literary assembly line. Every country has its national poetry; doubtless Luxembourg has its Shakespeare. But none of the others, chauvinism reassures us, can match ours. I still think that belief, drilled into me at school half a century ago, may have an element of truth.

Reading through the pages of Q's *OBEV*, one is superficially struck by the fact that so many of the poems are about – what else? – the English weather. The opening poem, a ballad (poetry of the people, and anonymous), is 'The Cuckoo Song', which is sometimes described as England's oldest surviving poem. 'The soul of Englishness', the folk-tale collector Andrew Lang called it. What follows is the oldest spelling version recorded:

> Sumer is icumen in,
> Lhude sing cuccu!

Groweþ sed and bloweþ med
And springþ þe wde nu,
Sing cuccu!

Awe bleteþ after lomb,
Lhouþ after calue cu.
Bulluc ſterteþ, bucke uerteþ,
Murie sing cuccu!

Cuccu, cuccu, wel singes þu cuccu;
Ne swik þu nauer nu.

Sing cuccu nu. Sing cuccu.
Sing cuccu. Sing cuccu nu!

Cynics will note that summer has not yet arrived; it's merely 'coming in'. There's usually more waiting than sunshine for those who live under the English weather.

The American poet and critic Ezra Pound, who came to England to teach his fellow American T. S. Eliot how to write modernist verse, concocted an ironic parody (reach for your brolly and galoshes, you soggy Englanders – your English weather is as dire as your Georgian poetry), picturing skidding buses, staining rain and the bawled-out refrain, 'Damn you, sing: Goddamn'. Whether 'Old Possum' (as Pound nicknamed Eliot) damned the weather of the nation he eventually joined is not recorded.

One can dip almost anywhere into the obev and find a weather forecast in verse, usually 'sun and showers', as the TV meteorologists say. But the poem that should glisten, for the Brexiteer, is Michael Drayton's seventeenth-century poem 'Agincourt'. It too starts with the vagaries of the English weather, but it goes on to render Shakespeare's *Henry V* in crystalline verse form. It fairly crows as it celebrates the valiant English, despite all odds against them, overthrowing the French ('a nation vile'). (Both Shakespeare and Drayton overlook the fact that King Hal, as they present him to us, is a war criminal who today would find himself on trial at The Hague, and most likely convicted, for slaughtering more than 1,000 French prisoners in his care because they were inconveniencing him.[43])

Fair ſtood the wind for France
When we our sails advance,
Nor now to prove our chance
 Longer will tarry;
 But putting to the main,
At Caux, the mouth of Seine,
With all his martial train
 Landed King Harry.

And taking many a fort,
Furnish'd in warlike sort,
Marcheth tow'rds Agincourt
 In happy hour;
Skirmishing day by day
With those that ſtopp'd his way,
Where the French gen'ral lay
 With all his power.

Which, in his height of pride,
King Henry to deride,
His ransom to provide
 Unto him sending;
Which he negleĉts the while
As from a nation vile,
Yet with an angry smile
 Their fall portending.

And turning to his men,
Quoth our brave Henry then,
'Though they to one be ten
    Be not amazèd:
Yet have we well begun;
Battles so bravely won
Have ever to the sun
    By fame been raisèd.

'And for myself (quoth he)
This my full reſt shall be:
England ne'er mourn for me
    Nor more eſteem me:
Victor I will remain
Or on this earth lie slain,
Never shall she suſtain
    Loss to redeem me.

'Poitiers and Cressy tell,
When moſt their pride did swell,
Under our swords they fell:
    No less our skill is
Than when our grandsire great,
Claiming the regal seat,
By many a warlike feat
    Lopp'd the French lilies.'

The Duke of York so dread
The eager vaward led;
With the main Henry sped
    Among his henchmen.
Exceſter had the rear,
A braver man not there;

O Lord, how hot they were
    On the false Frenchmen!

They now to fight are gone,
Armour on armour shone,
Drum now to drum did groan,
    To hear was wonder;
That with the cries they make
The very earth did shake:
Trumpet to trumpet spake,
    Thunder to thunder.

Well it thine age became,
O noble Erpingham,
Which didst the signal aim
    To our hid forces!
When from a meadow by,
Like a storm suddenly
The English archery
    Stuck the French horses.

With Spanish yew so strong,
Arrows a cloth-yard long
That like to serpents stung,
    Piercing the weather;
None from his fellow starts,
But playing manly parts,
And like true English hearts
    Stuck close together.

When down their bows they threw,
And forth their bilbos [swords] drew,
And on the French they flew,

Not one was tardy;
Arms were from shoulders sent,
Scalps to the teeth were rent,
Down the French peasants went –
    Our men were hardy.

This while our noble king,
His broadsword brandishing,
Down the French hoſt did ding
    As to o'erwhelm it;
And many a deep wound lent,
His arms with blood besprent,
And many a cruel dent
    Bruisèd his helmet.

Gloſter, that duke so good,
Next of the royal blood,
For famous England ſtood
    With his brave brother;
Clarence, in ſteel so bright,
Though but a maiden knight,
Yet in that furious fight
    Scarce such another.

Warwick in blood did wade,
Oxford the foe invade,
And cruel slaughter made
    Still as they ran up;
Suffolk his axe did ply,
Beaumont and Willoughby
Bare them right doughtily,
    Ferrers and Fanhope.

Upon Saint Crispin's Day
Fought was this noble fray,
Which fame did not delay
    To England to carry.
O when shall English men
With such acts fill a pen?
Or England breed again
    Such a King Harry?

A good question. It may be doggerel, but it is patriotic doggerel. The heart (under its tattooed red cross) swells reading it.

School Songsters

Drayton's poem can be found echoing through chauvinist literature for centuries afterwards. Only recently, with the end of empire, does it echo no more. It was a perennial favourite in the school classroom (it can be taken in by even the youngest child), and it was there, I recall, that as a schoolboy I first encountered it.

Drayton's influence penetrated into many school songs and was influential on the thinking they inculcated, along with *Hymns Ancient and Modern* at morning assembly. Young Nigel Farage attended Dulwich College in south London, whose school song is austerely Latinate (the school's curriculum, I've heard, isn't excessively so nowadays):

> *Pueri Alleynienses, quotquot annos quotquot menses*
> *Fertur principum memoria,*
> *Vivit Fundatoris nomen, unicae virtutis omen*
> *Detur soli Deo Gloria.*

It was composed by the school's Master in the high Victorian period, and has been Englished as

> Boys of Alleyn, may our forefathers' memory
> Endure through as many years and as many months
>   as there may be,
> The Founder's name lives on, a promise of unparalleled
>   virtue to come,
> Glory be given to God alone.[44]

The boy Nigel doubtless chanted it on ritual occasions. He has put down convincingly as outright slander the 'factoid' that circulated recently that he was given to ranting out Hitler Youth songs in south London's empty streets at midnight. Jugend will be Jugend.[45]

My own Colchester Royal Grammar School song, 'Carmen Colcestriense', as I recall it from the 1950s, has less Latin but a more rollicking lilt. It is a military quick-march song, not (like Dulwich's anthem to itself) a gloomy Gregorian chant:

> Now hands about for Colchester
> And sing a rousing chorus
> In praise of all our comrades here
> And those who went before us.
> For to this lay all hearts beat true;
> The loyal hearts that love us;
> So fortune fend each absent friend
> While there's a sun above us.
>
> *Chorus*:
> Sing! boys, sing!
> Floreat Sodalitas
> Little matter, well or ill,

Sentiment is more than skill,
Sing together with a will
Floreat Sodalitas
'tas Colceſtriensis

By mullioned panes the ivy climbs,
On Tudor masks and faces.
So mem'ry adds an evergreen
To well remembered places.
And grave oc's ſtill dream besides
Of days long since departed;
And some have expiated crimes
For which their backs have smarted!
(Chorus)

Tradition gives us pride of birth,
Brave hearts and gentle manners,
For we are sons of men who marched
Beneath the Tudor banners!
So as we pass the torch along
Aglow with high endeavour,
One kindly mother we acclaim
That she may ſtand for ever.

'For we are sons of men who marched/ Beneath the Tudor banners!': our forefathers were at Bosworth, young Colcestrians are to assume. With my name, I like to fantasize that some of mine were at Bannockburn as well – as unlikely, probably, as braveheart Mel Gibson's being there. Incidentally, I think Colchester's may be one of the few school songs to celebrate the sizzle of the master's cane on schoolboy rear ends. When I was at the school, only the headmaster was authorized to use the rattan – which, to his credit, he rarely did.[46]

The name of Percy Shaw Jeffrey (1862–1952), who wrote the song, has little currency outside the school gates behind which his anthem was bellowed out. He was a scholar (he did some minor work in phonetics) whose academic career was blighted by the fact that he got a third at Oxford. That sentence of scholarly excommunication from the dreaming spires meant a career lower down the social scale.

A man of parts, Shaw Jeffrey threw himself into schoolteaching, in the grammar schools that, in allegiance to Thomas Arnold of Rugby – who single-handedly created the modern public school system – tried hard to be public schools but weren't. The high point of Shaw Jeffrey's career was the sixteen years he spent at Colchester, from 1899 until his retirement. His main innovation as headmaster was to introduce day boys, over whose minds (I speak for myself) the Shaw Jeffrey school ethos (Rugby, rugby and cold showers) was less (de)formative. In honour of the royal foundation by Henry VIII, he introduced royal purple blazers (they literally did blaze) and peaked caps, which made CRGS 'grammar bugs' objects of vulgar contempt in the town ('eat slugs, dirty little hummerbugs', the oiks chanted at us, whenever purple hove into sight; I never did work out what that last word, 'hummerbugs', meant, although I heard it often enough). Inconveniently aged for either of the world wars he lived through – to his chagrin, one imagines, since one feels a martial spirit thumping in his ditty – Shaw Jeffrey retired in 1916 to South Africa, a country that was congenial to him with its thorough anglicization after the Boer War.

In 2006 I was invited to give the address at the school's speech day. Not, alas, on account of my schoolboy glory at CRGS, which was less than nil, or the books I had published (not one, I checked, was in the school library), but because I had recently been on *Desert Island Discs*, in which, as it happened, I had ventured some unnoticed uncomplimentary remarks about my alma mater.

My former school scores sky-high in league tables nowadays (sod 'sentiment is more than skill'). Did the boys still sing the school song? I asked the headmaster over the pre-event salmon-and-cress sandwiches. 'Didn't know we had one,' he replied jovially. *Sic transit.* No more ''tas Colcestriensis' at Colchester.

Brexiteers, Buccaneers, Musketeers; or, 'Up Yours, Señors!'

Muscular Christianity – Christianity with biceps – flourished in the 1850s, inflated by the Crimean War. This was the conflict that gave England the Charge of the Light Brigade, cigarettes (picked up from the Russian foe and Turkish allies; you couldn't charge into the valley of Death with twenty cigars stuffed in your ammunition pouches) and a decade-long fashion for heavy beards. 'Manly' was the approving word; face fungus the sneer.

Oddly, the thinking soldier's sex queen, the writer Ouida ('j'n'écris pour les femmes, j'écris pour les militaires'), was part of the 1850s war-loving vogue. It was she who immortalized the camp-follower heroine Cigarette, in love with the aristocratic hero who has joined France's foreign legions to forget. It popularized the gasper, which killed more people than the rifle ever did. Carlylean hero-worship was another main ingredient in Muscular Christianity, together with perennial prejudices about English racial purity. Spicing the ideological brew was a heavy dose of neo-Elizabethanism – something that boils up in the English psyche every generation or so, before subsiding out of sheer embarrassment.[47]

The leader and formulator of the Muscular Christianity creed, and a leading producer of its fiction, was Charles Kingsley with his bloodthirsty romance *Westward Ho!* (1855). The novel was specifically designed to whip up war fury among young British males for the adventure in the Crimea – one of the most pointless wars among the many Britain has chosen to lose British blood in. (British leaders rarely do nowadays.) He wrote the novel, said Kingsley (a clergyman), 'to make others fight' and to put 'brave thoughts' into England's mind.[48] He was himself too frail to pick up a musket, but he could think as bravely as Lionheart himself.

Westward Ho! was hugely popular in its own time, and for a century. It sank deep into the nation's psyche as a favourite school prize book, in which form I, as it happens, first read it.[49] Its hero is Amyas Leigh, a brutal young 'berserker' and a Devon man. We follow him from his schooldays (in which he beats up any schoolmaster who tries, foolishly, to 'master' him) to his first expedition around the world with the buccaneer Sir Francis Drake.

Leigh loves Rose Salterne, the beauty of Bideford, as do all the young men of the town. In chaste worship of her, they form 'the Brotherhood of the Rose'. Members vow that none of them will take advantage by wooing the maiden while their comrades are away on the high seas marketing slaves and piratically stealing Spanish gold (and doubtless doing naughty things in various ports of call. Even a berserker must have some R&R).

Leigh participates gleefully in the bloody eviction of the Spaniards from Ireland in 1580. There is a particularly nasty massacre of Spanish prisoners about which the narrator, Kingsley, serenely notes: 'the hint was severe, but it was sufficient. Many years passed before a Spaniard set foot again in Ireland.' Up yours, señors.[50]

A Spanish officer is taken prisoner and held at Bideford, awaiting ransom. He seduces and takes flight with Rose.[51] The Brotherhood follow in their ship, *The Rose*, and track the couple to South America, but it is too late. Rose has been martyred by the vile Spanish Inquisition for not renouncing her good English faith (Kingsley was a proselytizing Protestant Christian Socialist, for whom Catholicism was beyond satanic).

It all climaxes with the Armada, where, in his ship the *Vengeance*, Leigh pursues his Spanish foe and sees them perish in the great storm. *Deus afflavit*. Furious that he could not do the necessary murder himself, he curses God, who sends down a flash of lightning to blind the blasphemer. The Almighty too has muscles.

What relevance does this excessively bloodthirsty novel have for our time? *Westward Ho!*, for a certain generation (now in its fifties to seventies), still resonates. Liam Fox, one of the quartet of senior 'manly' politicos (let's call them a Brotherhood) charged by their nation to bring Brexit to pass, proclaimed: 'I yearn for those buccaneering pre-EU days, when Britain led the world in trade. And no one could record you on their phone.' Ah, yes, buccaneering days: where is the modern Drake when England needs him?

'Brexiteer brings to mind buccaneer, pioneer, musketeer,' echoed Michael Gove. 'It lends a sense of panache and romance to the argument.' Ex-SAS David Davis, another of the Brexit Brotherhood, embodies via his regiment the berserker spirit Kingsley admired. Legend has it the berserker would tie wet rawhide around his testicles to drive himself fighting mad as it dried. Some, of course, may think Mr Davis Brexit-berserk in another sense. Not I. Someone, I don't know who, digging deeper into nineteenth-century boys' romance, coined the term 'the three Brexiteers' for Fox, Davis and Gove – with uber-berserk Boris Johnson as a maverick fourth.

Westward Ho!'s Hispanophobia rings another bell. It was the spat over Gibraltar in 2017 that roused once more ancient English asperities against the 'dago'. Quite reasonably, the Spanish believe that an island a stone's throw from their southern coast might belong to them. Michael Howard (a prominent Leaver and former leader of the Conservative Party) thought otherwise in an interview with Sophy Ridge, after one of Spain's immigration office created, as they regularly do, traffic jams at the crossing point from island to mainland. 'Thirty-five years ago this week,' declared Howard,

> another woman prime minister sent a taskforce halfway across the world to defend the freedom of another small group of British people against another Spanish-speaking country, and I'm absolutely certain that our current prime minister will show the same resolve in standing by the people of Gibraltar.

In other words, watch it, señors!

Howard's 'thirty-five years' recalled, of course, the Iron Lady and the Falklands War. Buried underneath his defiance was a more distant allusion, to the Virgin Queen, whose navy (led, recall, by buccaneers) repulsed the Spanish Armada five hundred years ago – with a little gusty help from the Almighty.

Elizabethanism and Thatcherism are very dear to the Brexiteer. One of the literary works that is frequently invoked is Elizabeth's magnificent address to her people, and her sailors, at Tilbury. It is sometimes forgotten that Elizabeth is the only monarch of England who has any legitimate standing as a creative writer.[52] This is how (modernized) the Tilbury Address goes:

> My loving people,
> We have been persuaded by some that are careful of our safety, to take heed how we commit ourselves to armed multitudes, for fear of treachery; but I assure you I do not desire to live to distrust my faithful and loving people. Let tyrants fear, I have always so behaved myself

that, under God, I have placed my chiefest strength and safeguard in the loyal hearts and goodwill of my subjects; and therefore I am come amongst you, as you see, at this time, not for my recreation and disport, but being resolved, in the midst and heat of the battle, to live and die amongst you all; to lay down for my God, and for my kingdom, and my people, my honour and my blood, even in the dust.

I know I have the body but of a weak and feeble woman; but I have the heart and stomach of a king, and of a king of England too, and think foul scorn that Parma or Spain, or any prince of Europe, should dare to invade the borders of my realm; to which rather than any dishonour shall grow by me, I myself will take up arms, I myself will be your general, judge, and rewarder of every one of your virtues in the field.

I know already, for your forwardness you have deserved rewards and crowns; and We do assure you in the word of a prince, they shall be duly paid you. In the meantime, my lieutenant general shall be in my stead, than whom never prince commanded a more noble or worthy subject; not doubting but by your obedience to my general, by your concord in the camp, and your valour in the field, we shall shortly have a famous victory over those enemies of my God, of my kingdom, and of my people.

King Nigel I, one feels, could not have put it better. Let's hear it again: Up yours, señors! Right to the hilt.

Dickens, Anti-Brexiteer Extraordinaire

Charles Dickens had no time for the Crimean War. He saw it as a glaring example of civil service maladministration, leading to the unnecessary death of thousands of English soldiers. He was one of the founders of the Administrative Reform Association, which was aimed at reforming Whitehall (by getting rid of the nepotistically appointed Coodles, Doodles and Foodles, as he contemptuously calls them in *Bleak House*) into more acceptable efficiency. It resulted in the Northcote-Trevelyan reforms of the 1850s, by which intelligent people were recruited solely on the basis of their superior intelligence. Sir Humphrey of *Yes Minister* came into being. Dickens would also, one suspects, have had some bones to pick with Brexit, had he lived to see it. And that leads us (anachronistically) to Mr Podsnap.

It is always best to let Dickens speak for himself, since he is not a writer who likes to share what Theodore Roosevelt called 'the bully pulpit'. Sometimes, indeed, he is a novelist best read with mental earplugs. The following extract is the Great Inimitable's verbal cartoon of a minor character in *Our Mutual Friend* (1865), one of the masterpieces of his 'dark' period. John Podsnap is the fellow's name, and he is English to the marrow of his bones (and boneheadedness). Dickens's scorn for that kind of bourgeois Englishness is ineffable.

Podsnap has become as iconic a caricature as Mr Pickwick (who symbolizes, of course, a much nicer Englishness). Podsnappery, adversaries might say with a chortle, is Brexit *avant la lettre*. The following is an *Oxford Dictionary* definition: 'A person embodying insular complacency, self-satisfaction, and refusal to face up to unpleasant facts.' If the cap fits . . . This is how the abominable Mr Podsnap is introduced in Chapter Eleven of *Our Mutual Friend* (entitled 'Podsnappery'):

Mr Podsnap was well to do, and stood very high in Mr Podsnap's opinion. Beginning with a good inheritance, he had married a good inheritance, and had thriven exceedingly in the Marine Insurance way, and was quite satisfied. He never could make out why everybody was not quite satisfied, and he felt conscious that he set a brilliant social example in being particularly well satisfied with most things, and, above all other things, with himself.

Thus happily acquainted with his own merit and importance, Mr Podsnap settled that whatever he put behind him he put out of existence. There was a dignified conclusiveness – not to add a grand convenience – in this way of getting rid of disagreeables, which had done much towards establishing Mr Podsnap in his lofty place in Mr Podsnap's satisfaction. 'I don't want to know about it; I don't choose to discuss it; I don't admit it!' Mr Podsnap had even acquired a peculiar flourish of his right arm in often clearing the world of its most difficult problems, by sweeping them behind him (and consequently sheer away) with those words and a flushed face. For they affronted him.

Mr Podsnap's world was not a very large world, morally; no, nor even geographically: seeing that although his business was sustained upon commerce with other countries, he considered other countries, with that important reservation, a mistake, and of their manners and customs would conclusively observe, 'Not English!' when, PRESTO! with a flourish of the arm, and a flush of the face, they were swept away.

Dickens, it will be agreed, packs a hefty punch. But, if you're Brexit-inclined, before indignantly clapping your copy of *Our*

Mutual Friend shut, take on some biographical context. Dickens, who had no coherent school education, taught himself French: he was fluent and could write editorial letters in the language. In his younger days he and his uber-bohemian protégé Wilkie Collins liked to take short jaunts to Paris. What jinks, high or low, they got up to there are not recorded. Not, one suspects, daily visits to the Louvre and the Jardin des Plantes. In later life Dickens and his mistress Nelly went to live together in France, where their dalliance could remain private. They may, it is surmised, have had a child born there. Dickens, in short, was as cosmopolitan and Francophile (Europhile) in his chosen way as they come.

He could, of course, also be the Dickensian Francophobe, as in *A Tale of Two Cities* (1859), which is founded on a Carlylean disgust with the excesses of the Revolution, which was perceived as not English at all. Dickens's attitude to Europe was complex, and Dickensians still lock horns on the subject.

But Podsnap is as simple as mud. How should the Brexiteer take him? As a warning, I suggest, as an example of Brexitism gone a prejudice too far. Practise moderation in all things: appreciate the foreign, but with an appreciation founded on intelligent, not stupid, chauvinism. Nothing is simple.

Our National Anthem

On my Saturday night treat at the flicks as a child, I stood, like everyone else, when – the Hollywood (invariably) double bill having finished – the National Anthem was played. This is done no more, but it meant something important then, in the 1940s and 1950s. 'God Save the Queen' (as it was popularly called) stopped being played in cinemas around the early 1970s.

Followers of Brexit make the point that the EU may have anthems, but Brexiteers don't want to know them. It's an article of faith. How many English subjects (but not for long) of the Community could recite the words of Schiller's 'Ode to Joy', or know what the poem is on about. Joy? They can hum Beethoven's magnificent accompaniment, of course.

The British, more properly the English, National Anthem dates back to the eighteenth century. 'God Save the King' was first publicly performed in London in 1745 as the bare-arsed Scottish followers of Bonnie Prince Charlie were thundering down England, claymores swinging, after their victory at Prestonpans, with the aim of changing the Sassenach (or was he German) king, whatever God might think. The tune and words are anonymous. Legend has it that they were put together, as the metropolis trembled, by the band at the Theatre Royal in Drury Lane, and played after the performance. The anthem proved a huge success and, after publication in the *Gentleman's Magazine*, was established as a ritual at theatres, both live and film, until little John Sutherland got patriotically to his feet after watching, say, *The Dam Busters* or, more likely, the latest Abbott and Costello.

It became the 'National Anthem' in the early nineteenth century, and other nations followed suit, perceiving the usefulness of the institution. Some, including America, use the British tune for radically un-English sentiments ('My Country 'Tis of Thee'). Today, other than on 'occasions', with a choir in attendance, only the first verse is sung. Why that should be so is clear enough when one reads the subsequent disconcerting verses, concocted, recall, in haste 250 years ago (I have transgendered the monarch):

God save our gracious Queen!
Long live our noble Queen!
God save the Queen!
Send her victorious,
Happy and glorious,
Long to reign over us,
God save the Queen.

O Lord our God arise,
Scatter her enemies,
And make them fall.
Confound their politics,
Frustrate their knavish tricks,
On Thee our hopes we fix,
God save us all.

Thy choicest gifts in store
On her be pleased to pour,
Long may she reign.
May she defend our laws,
And ever give us cause,
To sing with heart and voice,
God save the Queen.

Not in this land alone,
But be God's mercies known
From shore to shore.
Lord make the nations see
That men should brothers be,
And form one family
The wide world over.
From every latent foe,
From the assassins blow

God save the Queen.
O'er her thine arm extend,
For Britain's sake defend
Our mother, prince, and friend,
God save the Queen.

Lord grant that Marshal Wade
May by thy mighty aid
Victory bring.
May he sedition hush,
And like a torrent rush
Rebellious Scots to crush,
God save the Queen.

I particularly like 'knavish tricks' – that fits the EU's doings perfectly. But who, one asks (and virtually everyone will have to), was Marshal Wade – the prospective saviour of the nation, if God, as petitioned in the first line, didn't do the saving first?

In the event, he wasn't England's saviour. Field Marshal George Wade failed signally to stop the Scottish horde rampaging down England. At the beginning of 1746 he was replaced as commander-in-chief by the Duke of Cumberland, who put a decisive end to the Scottish uprising at Culloden on 16 April that year. In England Cumberland, a notoriously brutal victor, gave his name to the flower sweet william; in Scotland he is memorialized in the weed stinking billy (ragwort). So much for the unity of the United Kingdom in the language of flowers.

Unsurprisingly, the National Anthem has never been a hit north of the border. In the 1990s *The Herald* ran a campaign to replace 'the racist, British Nationalist and anti-Scottish Anthem' with something authentically Caledonian. Devolved Scotland is still waiting.

Gibbon: The Congenital British *Non Serviam*

In 1789 Edward Gibbon published a big book about a big subject: the Roman Empire. More specifically, Imperial Rome's decline and fall. No other recorded empire has lasted as long as Rome's five hundred years, and the soldier and scholar Glubb Pasha (a wonderfully imperial name; he was known more humbly as John Bagot Glubb) reckoned the average run of empires was 350 years, give or take a century or two.[53] Our time was up, he concluded when he wrote his study *The Fate of Empires and Search for Survival* (1978). He turned out to be right.

The end of empire is accompanied, popular history affirms, by an unhealthy mix of warm baths, sexual laxity, self-indulgence (particularly when it comes to food) and enervation, and so the energy of the Goth, vandal and barbarian overcomes the late imperial will to fight and die for empire. Glubb adds the accession of female power as another disintegrating factor. Old empires do not die, or 'fade away' like old soldiers; they dissipate themselves into extinction. *Circumspice!*

Every imperial power declines and falls, and world history moves on forgetfully to empires new. Recall Shelley's poem 'Ozymandias' (1818) for the most beautiful statement of empire's temporariness and inevitable decline into oblivion:

I met a traveller from an antique land
Who said: 'Two vaſt and trunkless legs of ſtone
Stand in the desert ... Near them, on the sand,
Half sunk, a shattered visage lies, whose frown,
And wrinkled lip, and sneer of cold command,
Tell that its sculptor well those passions read
Which yet survive, ſtamped on these lifeless things,

The hand that mocked them, and the heart that fed:
And on the pedeſtal these words appear:
"My name is Ozymandias, king of kings:
Look on my works, ye Mighty, and despair!"
Nothing beside remains. Round the decay
Of that colossal wreck, boundless and bare
The lone and level sands ſtretch far away.'

Thus endeth all empire.[54] Buried, unremembered, in the sands of time. Inspiration came to Gibbon in just such an Ozymandian moment, beautifully recorded: 'It was at Rome, on the fifteenth of October 1764, as I sat musing amidst the ruins of the Capitol, while the barefoot friars were singing vespers in the Temple of Jupiter, that the idea of writing the decline and fall of the city first started to my mind.' The EU has, it is assumed, quasi-imperial status and allegedly (some think) aspires to full empiredom. With luck, once it achieves that grandeur it may survive the Glubbian 3.5 centuries. Not every Brexiteer wishes it luck.

Gibbonian prose is so Augustan that the eye glissades effortlessly over the page. Messages to the attentive reader are, however, dropped everywhere. The thoughtful Brexiteer can linger profitably on the following passage from Gibbon's prelude, which deals with the awkward imperial conquest of ancient Britain by Rome in the first century AD. It was not as easy as other territorial occupations. Why? Because England – even in these ancient times – spurns the invader and occupier. Up yours, Caesar! Gibbon puts it more mellifluously:

The only accession which the Roman empire received, during the firſt century of the Chriſtian Aera, was the province of Britain. In this single inſtance, the succes-sors of Caesar and Auguſtus were persuaded to follow the example of the former, rather than the precept of the latter. The proximity of its situation to the coast of Gaul seemed to invite their arms; the pleasing though doubtful intelligence of a pearl fishery, attracted their avarice; and as Britain was viewed in the light of a distinct and insulated world, the conquest scarcely formed any exception to the general system of continental measures. After a war of about forty years, undertaken by the most stupid, maintained by the most dissolute, and terminated by the most timid of all the emperors, the far greater part of the island submitted to the Roman yoke. The various tribes of Britain possessed valour without conduct, and the love of freedom without the spirit of union. They took up arms with savage fierceness; they laid them down, *or turned them against each other, with wild inconsistency; and while they fought singly, they were successively subdued.* Neither the fortitude of Caractacus, nor the despair of Boadicea, nor the fanaticism of the Druids, could avert the slavery of their country, or resist the steady progress of the Imperial generals, who maintained the national glory, when the throne was disgraced by the weakest, or the most vicious of mankind. [my emphasis]

There is food for Brexitian thought here, not least how consistently bolshy the English character has been over the centuries. It has been especially so as regards domination from outside, whether the dominator be Imperial Rome, the Vatican or, since 1973, Brussels. One can be proud of that.

But the danger Gibbon points to is that the British also inveterately squabble among themselves, and in so doing are constantly in danger of losing what they gained in the fights they have won. 'Wild inconsistency', he calls it; one step forward, two steps back. The English are notoriously unable to join forces with each other – the Iceni, for example, never put their formidable martial energies into forming an English nation. There has always been a big question mark over the 'U' in UK.

One moral I draw from this jewel of Gibbonian prose is that if Brexit, as a cause, really wants to last, hatchets should be buried. No more intranational insults about 'Remoaners' (odious compound), no more combat not against the opponent, but against deviants in English ranks. Transcending tribalism must be the order of the day. Think big; think unified. I suspect Brexit may find that difficult.

Ivanhoe and the Norman Yoke

Nigel Farage's resentment of the Norman Invasion, after nine hundred years, has been mentioned, specifically with reference to his Bayeux Tapestry tie. He wore it, he quipped, to recall 'the last time we were invaded and taken over'. Farage is manifestly a subscriber to what historians call the Norman Yoke thesis.

Many English commentators have deplored the so-called Norman Yoke. The eighteenth-century political theorist Thomas Paine, for example, described the Conqueror as a 'French bastard landing with armed banditti' who went on to steal and enslave a country that wasn't theirs.

It was Walter Scott who put wings on the thesis. The novel in which he did so, *Ivanhoe* (1820), should have a proud, much-thumbed place in every Brexit bookcase. The narrative is set in England, 130 years after the Conquest, with the indigenous Saxons still writhing under the Norman heel. 'Four generations', Scott ruefully records, had not sufficed to blend the hostile blood of the Normans and Anglo-Saxons, or to unite, by common language and mutual interests, two hostile races, one of which still felt the elation of triumph, while the other groaned under all the consequences of defeat. The power had been completely placed in the hands of the Norman nobility, by the event of the battle of Hastings, and it had been used, as our histories assure us, with no moderate hand. The whole race of Saxon princes and nobles had been extirpated or disinherited, with few or no exceptions; nor were the numbers great who possessed land in the country of their fathers, even as proprietors of the second, or of yet inferior classes.

Enter to the rescue of England Robin Hood (a rather classier *banditto* than those of William's crew), Sir Wilfred of Ivanhoe (son of Cedric the Saxon) and Richard the Lionheart (just back from biffing the Muslims in the Third Crusade) – a formidable team.

I will ignore Scott's grand narrative, readable as it is, to concentrate on one small but telling episode. The Anglo-Normans, as masters of England, ate higher on the *cochon* than the handfuls of Hastings sand William had allegedly gobbled down on his arrival. To the England they stole they brought France's great invention: *cuisine*.

Ivanhoe opens, after Scott's preamble (he always, incidentally, got the story going on page 50, after a long winding up), with a couple of Saxon oiks, Gurth and Wamba, chatting aimlessly and munching their meagre victuals in the woods. Gurth, sitting on a 'fallen Druidical monument' (a nice Ozymandian touch), is a swineherd; Wamba, 'the son of Witless', is a clown or jester – a witty fool. Wamba quizzes his dull friend with a gesture at the animals he is tending:

'Why, how call you those grunting brutes running about on their four legs?' demanded Wamba.

'Swine, fool, swine,' said the herd, 'every fool knows that.'

'And swine is good Saxon,' said the jester; 'but how call you the sow when she is flayed, and drawn, and quartered, and hung up by the heels like a traitor?'

'Pork,' answered the swineherd.

'I am very glad every fool knows that too,' said Wamba, 'and pork, I think, is good Norman-French; and so when the brute lives, and is in the charge of a Saxon slave, she goes by her Saxon name; but becomes a Norman, and is called pork, when she is carried to the Castle-hall to feast among the nobles.'

It's not just swine/pork. Sheep flesh is 'mutton' (*mouton*) on the Anglo-Norman table, cow-meat is 'beef' (*boeuf*) and chicken *coq*. The Norman masters see their meat (including *cheval*) 'dressed' on the table, not grazing and defecating in the field. Throw off that Norman Yoke! Scott's novel enjoins. Pig trotters, chitterlings and cow pie for supper, or haggis (*andouil- lette*, as the Normans call it), whose ingredients it is best for the English palate not to be too curious about.

But alas, no. If there is one place where the Norman Yoke endures to this day it is in the upmarket restaurant. No cow pie (Desperate Dan's favourite chow) there, *mon ami*. I quote from my (and the late Lucian Freud's) favourite London restaurant's dinner menu:[55]

Entrées

Soufflé Suisse £12.75
Coq au Vin *for one* £19.75 *for two* £38.50
Choucroute à l'Alsacienne £18.25

Roaſt Anjou Chicken *ratatouille and herb oil* £21.50
Navarin of Lamb *summer vegetables and rosemary* £23.00

Every time I pass even the humble Prêt à Manger I feel that damned yoke chafing my shoulders.

Postscript: Brentry

There is a counter-argument about the Norman Yoke, which every Brexiteer should take on board, if only to confute it. Lucidly put by an anonymous writer on *The Economist*, in that journal's Christmas 2016 issue, it wasn't a 'yoke' that 1066 laid on English shoulders, but the apparatus of a fully functioning nation:

> But, while the blood and guts were horrifying, the conqueſt also did a lot of good. It transformed the English economy. Inſtitutions, trade patterns and inveſtment all improved. It brought some of the British Isles into European circles of trade ('Brentry', if you will) and sparked a long economic boom in England which made the country comparatively rich. The conqueſt and its aftermath also set a wealthy south apart from a poor north, a geographical divide that continues to this day. From those tumultuous decades on, England was indelibly European – and a lot ſtronger for it. The Norman conqueſt made England.

The 1066 Norman Brentry established our modern banking, loan and credit systems, allied organically with those of Europe. Jewish financiers arrived at William's specific invitation and introduced a network of credit links between his new English lands and his old French estates. Unhindered by Christian usury laws, Jews were the predominant lenders in England by the thirteenth century (see Isaac of York in *Ivanhoe*), and that credit allowed the creation of a material and bureaucratic infrastructure. If you want to tax a country, you must organize it first.

William was a tyrant, as was his entourage. I know no fiction like *Ivanhoe* for glorifying or romanticizing the Conqueror and his crew of *banditti*. But he has some claim to having made England a modern state, and, of course, giving us *Choucroute à l'Alsacienne*. What, then, should be the Brexit reply? 'Thank you very much, Monsieur, and now we can get on very well ourselves. And leave those two mouthfuls of sand, if you please.'

Jane Austen's 'England'

The year 2016 was Shakespeare's; 2017 was Jane Austen's. In that year Austen, whose reputation had risen over recent decades to near Shakespearian levels, joined that select band of writers who have featured on coin of the realm. Specifically, a quite appalling portrait of her ornaments England's new tenner. Ironically, that is the sum she got from her first publisher – who then chose not to publish her book.[56]

Austen's novels are a treasure house, but there is not a lot of direct relevance for the Brexit-interested reader. Something can be found, glancingly, however, in one of the most famous episodes in her fiction: the Donwell Abbey picnic in *Emma*. The picnickers, with nothing much to say to each other, and rather enervated by the summer heat, wander off to drink in the view. Of particular interest to Emma is Abbey Mill Farm, where her friend Harriet Smith ('the natural daughter of nobody knows whom') once expected to live as farmer Robert Martin's wife. Emma's mind then ranges over larger topics:

It was hot; and after walking some time over the gardens in a scattered, dispersed way, scarcely any three together, they insensibly followed one another to the delicious shade of a broad short avenue of limes, which ſtretching beyond the garden at an equal diſtance from the river, seemed the finish of the pleasure grounds. It led to nothing; nothing but a view at the end over a low ſtone wall with high pillars, which seemed intended, in their erection, to give the appearance of an approach to the house, which never had been there. Disputable, however, as might be the taſte of such a termination, it was in itself a charming walk, and the view which closed it extremely pretty. The considerable slope, at nearly the foot of which the Abbey ſtood, gradually acquired a ſteeper form beyond its grounds; and at half a mile diſtant was a bank of considerable abruptness and grandeur, well clothed with wood; and at the bottom of this bank, favourably placed and sheltered, rose the Abbey Mill Farm, with meadows in front, and the river making a close and handsome curve around it.

It was a sweet view – sweet to the eye and the mind. *English verdure, English culture, English comfort*, seen under a sun bright, without being oppressive. [my emphasis]

What is Austen saying here, particularly in her encomium of the 'Englishness' of the scene? She was a writer 'who only England knew'. She had sailor brothers who had seen the world, but not Jane, who never left England's shores (except, perhaps, for the adjoining Isle of Wight). A visit to Lyme Regis was a great thing. Miss Austen was bottled up in England like a wasp in a jam jar. There is not a single foreigner, as I recall, in any of her six novels, to bring with them witness of faraway places (occasionally, characters like the sea-going Crofts in *Persuasian* talk about far-flung countries). And yet Jane has this serene confidence that her country is the best anywhere. What is this superior 'English verdure, English culture, English comfort'? For the English monks whose Donwell Abbey was despoiled in the Reformation, England must have been very uncomfortable. Ruined abbeys, as did Thomas Carlyle in *Past and Present* (1843), stimulated thought about what had been lost of Olde England, and what might still be retained (when the referendum goes our way, we might add). If Robert Martin is working in the fields on this hot summer's day, he may not be exactly 'comfortable'.[57]

The clue, as always with Austen, is in the implication of the language she uses, in what runs beneath the surface of her words. Consider again those ringing nouns 'verdure; culture; comfort'.[58] They are, beneath their skimpy anglicization, French words, *verdure, culture, confort*. Why not, for example, 'greenery' instead of 'verdure'? It would trip off the tongue as easily. 'Verdure' would, by contrast, trip easily off the tongue of William the Conqueror: 'J'aime beaucoup le verdure de cette ville "Ahstins". Nous aurions grands conforts ici, mes braves.'

An answer can be found in dates. The novel was written in 1814–15, ominous years for English–French relations, with Waterloo, Napoleon's exile, victory, then peace and the inauguration of the 'British Century'. Not even a parson's daughter in rural Hampshire could be unaware that the world was changing.

Austen knew that, as Wellington put it, England's victory was a 'damn close-run thing', since she lived in a household that was highly literate and *au courant* with what was going on abroad. With Napoleon foiled, England had pulled it off – ring the church bells till your ears ache! For Austen's whole conscious lifetime, her country had been at war with France and – in their hearts – terrified that something like the Revolution could happen in England. Despite recent arguments to the contrary, it seems self-evident that Austen was anti-Jacobin in the political sentiments that are the invisible foundation of her comedy.[59]

To have written 'English greenery, English farming, English peacefulness' would have been insipid. It wouldn't have had what Thatcher called the 'rejoice' factor after the Falklands victory. More importantly, it would fail in Austen's subversive purpose: to raise a personal hip-hip at successful English resistance to a second French conquest.

How, one goes on to ask, would Austen have voted on 23 June 2016, two centuries on from *Emma*? The answer is in that thrice-repeated epithet 'English'.[60]

W. E. Henley

William Ernest Henley, one of the many forgotten of British Victorian literature, had a posthumous flash of fame in the 1990s. One of the things that had kept him going during his weary years in Robben Island, Nelson Mandela confided to the world, was Henley's poem 'Invictus', the 'unconquered', notably the final, defiant verse about what durance vile could never touch:

> It matters not how ſtrait the gate,
> How charged with punishments the scroll,
> I am the maſter of my fate:
> I am the captain of my soul.

As Wikipedia bleakly notes, Henley's literary reputation nowadays rests almost entirely upon this single poem and Mandela's endorsement of it. Henley wrote 'Invictus' in hospital, with the prospect of losing one or both legs to bone tuberculosis.

A different kind of defiance from Mandela's was required. Henley lost one limb. Oddly, extrapulmonary tuberculosis does not have the literary glamour of the 'poet's disease', which goes for the lungs.

Henley's name crops up often in connection with his friend Robert Louis Stevenson, whose lungs were going the same way as Henley's legs. Stevenson immortalized Henley as Long John Silver. Henley was the least crippled of men in everything apart from what Peter Cook might have called his 'one leg too few'.

Despite the Wikipedia verdict, another poem of Henley's is of interest: 'Pro Rege Nostro' ('for our realm' – Henley liked grandiose Latin titles and patriotic sentiments). Certain of the lines will sound familiar; they often crop up when Brexit is the subject:

> What have I done for you,
>   England, my England?
> What is there I would not do,
>   England, my own?
> With your glorious eyes austere,
> As the Lord were walking near,
> Whispering terrible things and dear
>   As the Song on your bugles blown,
>   England –
> Round the world on your bugles blown!

> Where shall the watchful Sun,
>   England, my England,
> Match the master-work you've done,
>   England, my own?
> When shall he rejoice agen
> Such a breed of mighty men

As come forward, one to ten,
   To the Song on your bugles blown,
      England –
   Down the years on your bugles blown?

Ever the faith endures,
   England, my England: –
'Take and break us: we are yours,
   England, my own!
'Life is good, and joy runs high
'Between English earth and sky:
'Death is death; but we shall die
   'To the Song on your bugles blown,
      'England –
   'To the stars on your bugles blown!'

They call you proud and hard,
   England, my England:
You with worlds to watch and ward,
   England, my own!
You whose mailed hand keeps the keys
Of such teeming destinies,
You could know nor dread nor ease,
   Were the Song on your bugles blown,
      England –
   Round the Pit on your bugles blown!

Mother of Ships whose might,
   England, my England,
Is the fierce old Sea's delight,
   England, my own,
Chosen daughter of the Lord,
Spouse-in-Chief of the ancient Sword,

> There's the menace of the Word
>   In the Song on your bugles blown,
>   England –
>   Out of heaven on your bugles blown!

Twenty mentions of 'England' in fifty lines. Is it a record?

'Pro Rege Nostro' was set to music as 'England, My England'. It was originally published among a pro-Boer War collection of poems in 1900. Much as he revered 'Invictus', Nelson Mandela would not have liked that connection, had he known about it. The Boer War was, among other things, a battle for who owned the right to exploit South Africa's indigenous population – the 'Kaffirs', as their colonial masters insultingly called them.

'Pro Rege Nostro' has a prominent place in Arthur Quiller-Couch's above-mentioned *Oxford Book of English Verse*. The martial quality of the poem rendered it popular among British soldiers (less so, perhaps, among the Irish, Welsh and Scots regiments) in the First World War. The poem poses the question what, if push came to shove, would one 'give' (meaning offer) for England? One's vote, perhaps – a cross on a sheet of paper. But what if that cross, and millions alongside it, led one to lose one's job? One's right arm epidermis for a tattoo? Unerasable. But one's life? Or even one's leg(s)? At that point the stakes become very high.

My father made 'the ultimate sacrifice' in the Second World War. But was he, born a Scot, giving up at 26 his future existence for 'England', or for something else? He wasn't running away from anything. He loved his wife, his job and – I like to think – baby me. He volunteered. As an overage London policeman, he would not have been called up unless the war went very badly wrong, which it didn't. But for him it went very badly wrong indeed. I never knew him; I cannot remember his face, other than from photographs, and even they are fading now.

Is there, was there, ever an actual 'England' worth my father's dying for? Or is that idea of an England worth the ultimate sacrifice what Henrik Ibsen calls a 'life-lie'?[61]

What if – to indulge in counterfactual history – after June 2016 the EU, inspired by the memory of Napoleon, had mustered a rapid reaction force to invade *perfide Albion* and bring her to her senses? How many in that fanciful scenario would have fought the enemy on the beaches, Churchill-style? How many of the English population today would give their 'all' for their country, as my father and hundreds of thousands of others like him did?

Henley's poetry is rousing but, posterity judges, second-rate as literature – which is why one doesn't find him on any A-level syllabus. Thanks to Mandela, there may be some educational spotlight on the author of 'Invictus' for a year or two. Nonetheless, the question Henley asks, transposed to the present, is a powerful one: 'You want Brexit? How much are you prepared to give for it?' Forget that hundred million euro divorce bill. We are talking blood.

Rivers of Blood Wash over our Green and Pleasant Land

Why give up a thousand years of struggle for our self government and discard our independence and submit to laws passed by foreigners?

That was Enoch Powell's question on the eve of the UK's voting to stay in the Common Market, in 1975, two years after joining. He foresaw the marketplace's evolution into the Frankensteinian-monstrous superstate the 'European Union'. Soothsayer Enoch.

If there is one dead body around which the roots of Brexit clutch and from which they draw nourishment, it is that of Powell, who was formative of what evolved into UKIP. His view of union of any kind with Europe was unwaveringly ferocious. In an interview with Robin Day during the count after the decisive referendum in 1975, Powell – who never, supposedly, spoke publicly without an overfull bladder – was apocalyptic. I saw the programme: Day was left dumbfounded (and me; I'd voted to stay in):

> POWELL: This is like September 1938. In September, October 1938 I'm sure that, if Neville Chamberlain had gone to the country, he would have swept the country for an act of abnegation. But the very same people, within 12 months, when they saw behind the facade, when they penetrated to the realities, stood up to fight for the continued existence of our nation; and that's what will happen.
> DAY: You're saying that this is a kind of Munich?
> POWELL: Yes I am.

Powell, alas, was dead before the people's great dissent from the 'Munich' of 1975 happened in 2016. He would scarcely have been able to retain his urine for pleasure.

AS A SCHOOLBOY, Nigel Farage recalls first hearing his hero (then and now) speak at Dulwich College. He was 'dazzled' and 'awestruck'.[62] The Enochian dazzle never faded for Nigel, boy and man. In 1994 he asked for Powell's endorsement in his first attempt on Parliament, in Eastleigh.[63] Powell himself was later invited to be a UKIP candidate, but there was no hope there: enfeebled by Parkinson's, in his eighties, he was no longer a public man. His bladder could now rest. He did, however, intimate moral support. Farage went on record himself in 2008 as admiring Powell whatever his obnoxious views on race: 'While his language may seem out of date now, the principles remain good and true.' Language?

Powell's pose as a public figure was dramatic, and classicist. He took it on himself to warn the country as a truth-telling Cassandra, cursed by the Gods not to be listened to. Powell was one of the few members of the House who could have recited Cassandra's curse in Homer's Greek; as an undergraduate at Cambridge he had swept the board of every classical prize available to him. His tutor was the classicist and English poet A. E. Housman, whose insularity and scorn for lesser minds were a lastingly powerful influence on his brilliant pupil. Powell went on to become a full professor of classics at the University of Sydney aged 25, a rank normally reached at that time by a few lucky academics, at twice the age. The Second World War discontinued Powell's academic career, and he never returned to the ivory tower (although there was always an invisible mortar board over his head). He rose to brigadier, then turned to politics.

I met Powell to talk to once, in the cellars (if I remember correctly) of Westminster Abbey in 1994. A colleague had just published the authoritative biography of William Tyndale, and, after what the country had done to Tyndale (burned him alive), it seemed an appropriate place for the book launch. Powell himself had suffered a kind of political execution. We exchanged some words about Tyndale and the King James Bible the great Englisher inspired. Powell knew more than me, I discovered; he knew more about everything than everyone. And little good it ultimately did him.

Powell was marinated in high literature, principally English and classics. He himself wrote poetry, in the Housman/Hardy plain-man's style, a worthily 'English' style. Modernism appealed to him even less than did Europe. It is helpful here to read one of his early poems, published in his first slim volume, in 1938, with war looming. The enjambement is, I think, cunning. The echo of Rupert Brooke in the title ('If I should die, think only this of me') is historically apposite and intended. The notion of his returning as a ghost to haunt his mother strikes a rather unsettling note, as does the image of embryonic Enoch waiting impatiently in his mother's lower parts to get out and do things:

> When I am gone, remember me,
> Not often. But when in the east
> Grey light is growing, and the mind
> With fears and hope is clouded least.
> Then in the hour that I love best,
> And where I still reflected find,
> All that I ever sought to be,
> I will return to you as one
> New risen from the grave, as clear
> As now you see me and as dear
> As when I slept beneath your breast
> Before I saw the sun.

I like the poem, although there is nothing Brexit-relevant in it. Two Powellite catchphrases from the poetry of others have, however, been sloganized and adopted into foundational UKIP/ Brexit creed.

As regards the first, 'rivers of blood', Mary Beard, in a thoughtful blog for the *Times Literary Supplement* on 5 November 2007, pondered Powell's notorious speech of 1968, pointing out that

> Powell never actually used the phrase 'Rivers of Blood'...
> The closest [he] came to it was a famous, but significantly

different, quote from Virgil's *Aeneid* ... What he actually said was 'like the Roman, I seem to see "the River Tiber foaming with much blood."' – in other words he's using Virgil, *Aeneid* VI, 87, a quote that comes half way through that great epic on Rome's foundation by the Trojan refugee Aeneas.

The words were spoken by the prophetic priestess, the Sibyl from Cumae ... She was prophesying the battles that Aeneas would face with the indigenous peoples of Italy before he would be able to found his brand new, multicultural city ... Virgil was offering a long-term message about ethnically mixed States: Rome would become a joint, shared community after all the bloodshed. But this was not what Powell had in mind. He was, I imagine, exploiting this quote because it was spoken by a divine prophetess who knew the truth about the future: he was going for classical legitimation for his *own* Sibylline prophecy about immigration.

It's a donnishly instructive quibble. And, of course, we're still waiting for that red foaming stain in Old Father Thames.

There are, it should be said, occasions when Powell is quite forthright; he was not one to mince words. So potent was his expression that a group of admirers set up the Churchill Society. Powell's fan club, one might call them. The society was founded in commemoration of a speech Powell gave on St George's Day, 1961. It is worth quoting at some length – if only because it expresses, with an oratorical lucidity none of the movement's current supporters could now match, a core sentiment of Brexit.

There was a saying, not heard today so often as formerly ... 'What do they know of England who only England know?'[64]

It is a saying which dates. It has a period aroma, like Kipling's 'Recessional' or the ſtaterooms at Osborne [House]. That phase is ended, so plainly ended, that even the generation born at its zenith, for whom the realization is the hardeſt, no longer deceive themselves as to the faᑐt. That power and that glory have vanished, as surely, if not as tracelessly, as the imperial fleet from the waters of Spithead.

And yet England is not as Nineveh and Tyre, nor as Rome, nor as Spain. Herodotus relates how the Athenians, returning to their city after it had been sacked and burnt by Xerxes and the Persian army, were aſtonished to find, alive and flourishing in the blackened ruins, the sacred olive tree, the native symbol of their country.

So we today, at the heart of a vanished empire, amid the fragments of demolished glory, seem to find, like one of her own oak trees, ſtanding and growing, the sap ſtill rising from her ancient roots to meet the spring, England herself.

Perhaps, after all, we know moſt of England 'who only England know'.

. . . For the unbroken life of the English nation over a thousand years and more is a phenomenon unique in hiſtory, the produᑐt of a specific set of circumſtances like those which in biology are supposed to ſtart by chance a new line of evolution. Inſtitutions which elsewhere are recent and artificial creations appear in England almoſt as works of nature, spontaneous and unqueſtioned.

From this continuous life of a united people in its island home spring, as from the soil of England, all that is peculiar in the gifts and the achievements of the English nation. All its impaᑐt on the outer world in earlier colonies, in the later Pax Britannica, in government and lawgiving, in commerce and in thought has flowed from impulses generated here. And this continuing life of England is symbolized and expressed, as by nothing else, by the English kingship. English it is, for all the leeks and thistles grafted upon it here and elsewhere. The stock that received all these grafts is English; the sap that rises through it to the extremities rises from roots in English earth, the earth of England's history.

As oratory, it doubtless blew away those of like mind in 1961. Powell has some legitimate claim to be the twentieth-century Demosthenes; only his close friend the socialist Michael Foot was his equal oratorically in the House or on the hustings. But what is interesting is Powell's use of literary reference to support his argument. He – unlike the present generation of Brexiteers – knew English, and classical, literary history as a scholar knows it. And, we infer, it had formed his unusually brilliant, if wayward, mind.

Postscript: Kipling's 'The English Flag'

Kipling's Barrack Room Ballad 'The English Flag' is the allusion on which Powell's 1961 speech pivots. The poem, first published in 1891, is essentially a plea for the working class ('little street-bred people') to buck themselves up and give their all for their country, its empire and the empire's inexorable expansion, east, south, north and west. The big things. Kipling is enraged (as was Powell in 1975) at the English working class's refusal to knuckle down and do what history and, more importantly, England expected of them. I quote Kipling's first stanza ('They' in the first line is the recalcitrant underclass unwilling to go out and die for the flag):

Winds of the World, give answer! They are whimpering
    to and fro –
And what should they know of England who only
    England know? –
The poor little ſtreet-bred people that vapour and
    fume and brag,
They are lifting their heads in the ſtillness to yelp at
    the English Flag!

If only these 'little street-bred people' could see, with their eyes or in their mind, a bit more of the world (that vast chunk coloured red), the 'people' would understand and follow their destiny: to die for the flag.

Brexit's Green and Pleasant Land

Powell quoted the phrase 'green and pleasant land' often, and it has stuck to his image like Sellotape. He used it in the so-called Rivers of Blood speech. It comes up, ritually, in UKIP/ Brexit discourse. It was the leitmotif in Danny Boyle's opening, and nakedly socialist, ceremony for the 2012 Olympics, with the assertion to the watching world's billions that England (and the NHS) is Edenic. Or, at least, green and pleasant.

Sometimes the phrase is trotted out as unadulterated chauvinism, as meaningless as a patriotic belch. William Blake's poem 'Jerusalem', from which it comes, is bellowed out, with much waving of Union Jacks, at the Last Night of the Proms each year. Parry's musical version of 'Jerusalem' was composed and first performed, for public singing, in 1916, at the height of the First World War. Although Brexit has made most frequent recent use of it, Blake's poem means all things to all parties. David Cameron, for example, supported the idea of 'Jerusalem' as the national anthem for British sports teams (green and pleasant Wimbledon lawn? Wembley turf?).[65]

Common usage of the phrase is typically based on misreading and simplification. But, consistently, there is the sense that this one poem expresses something quintessentially English, as it does in the climax of the movie *Chariots of Fire* (1981) and its theme that we Britons sprint differently from the rest of the world. More Britishly. That may be why we lose so often.

The phrase trips frequently off Nigel Farage's tongue, most memorably in his anathema about wind farms in 2013 (dare one picture Don Nigel tilting quixotically against electricity-generating windmills? Perish the thought): 'I'd like to blow them all up. I don't think I've ever seen a single issue in my life more insanely stupid than despoiling our green and pleasant land and our seascapes with ugly bird- and bat-chomping monsters that don't work.'[66]

'Jerusalem', to insist on the point, is a work of literature that should be cherished by every literate Brexiteer – if only by title and in partial quotation, with or without the orchestral oompah oompah. It says, one feels, what 'Brexit' means. The problem is that no one, not even the pointy-headed professoriate, knows *quite* what Blake is getting at in it. This is how it goes:

> And did those feet in ancient time
> Walk upon England's mountains green?
> And was the holy Lamb of God
> On England's pleasant pastures seen?
>
> And did the Countenance Divine
> Shine forth upon our clouded hills?
> And was Jerusalem builded here
> Among these dark Satanic Mills?

Bring me my bow of burning gold!
Bring me my arrows of desire!
Bring me my spear! O clouds, unfold!
Bring me my chariot of fire!

I will not cease from mental fight,
Nor shall my sword sleep in my hand,
Till we have built Jerusalem
In England's green and pleasant land.

Answer, without recourse to Wikipedia or any scholarly annotation, the following questions:

Q1: Whose feet are we talking about? And why?
Q2: What exactly are the 'dark Satanic Mills'?
Q3: What are the 'arrows of desire'?

'Jerusalem' is a beautifully misty poem, out of whose swirls no one emerges quite sure where they have been. But for the Good Brexiteer, the poem is an intravenous connection with their GOM, Enoch Powell. The famous four words are enough to carry essential UKIP baggage. Brexit likes to travel light. The great thing about literary touchstones, said Matthew Arnold, is that they are small enough to carry and caress in the pocket. Green and pleasant land is an emerald touchstone.

And the answers to those questions:

A1: Those of Jesus Christ. Legend, wholly apocryphal, has it that the Saviour visited ancient Britain – shoeless, apparently. An illegal immigrant, dare one say?
A2: There is fevered discussion about this. The mills are, best interpretation suggests, not factories but Anglican churches. Thought for the day.

A3: Sexual luſt. Blake believed in libido as a force for good. The 1960s would, however, be a long wait.

A. E. Housman and Thomas Hardy

There is, as noted above, an apostolic line linking Nigel Farage to Enoch Powell and Enoch Powell back to his Cambridge tutor, A. E. Housman. Peter Parker's biography of the poet, published, and applauded, a few weeks after the referendum of 2016, is entitled *Housman Country: Into the Heart of England*. Blake Morrison, poet and critic, opened his *Guardian* review of Parker's book thus:

> It's easy to see why A. E. Housman might appeal to supporters of Brexit. With his deep attachment to England and its countryside, he evokes the same feelings the out lobby played on: pride, patriotism and noſtalgia for the kind of unspoilt landscape – ſtreams, farms, woods, spires, green paſtures and windy wealds – that people think of as quintessentially English. Such sentiments, Peter Parker remarks in this excellent book, have become a 'comfort blanket for adults in which they can wrap themselves againſt the chill winds of the present'. But as he points out, Housman's poems, closely read, offer no such consolation. The 'land of loſt content' will never be regained; its 'blue remembered hills' exiſt only in the memory; its 'happy highways' are ones to which we 'cannot come again'.

The following verse from *A Shropshire Lad* is what Morrison is referring to:

Into my heart on air that kills
From yon far country blows:
What are those blue remembered hills,
What spires, what farms are those?
That is the land of lost content,
I see it shining plain,
The happy highways where I went
And cannot come again.

One of the more intractable issues for the thoughtfully literate Brexiteer is the problem enunciated over and over again in Housman's poetry: past England is lost; can it be recovered? It is unnecessary to stress the point that Brexit thinking is suffused with nostalgia. 'Sovereignty' – one of the movement's keywords – is more at home in Shakespeare's history plays than relevant today, when sovereigns no more run the country than bonnet mascots run cars.

Brexit is, at its core, desperate to bring back Old England, and vindicate it. The majority of the British people, as the vote of June 2016 witnessed, are of the same mind. Quixotic is again the word.

The Man of Wessex

In this poetic postlude there is another poet to point to: Thomas Hardy. Every Brexiteer should relish Hardy. He is a poet who, like Housman, looked inwards to England and backwards to the oldest England he felt living contact with. He called it Wessex, an Anglo-Saxon name for what weather forecasters blandly call the 'South West'.

One of Hardy's most anthologized poems, 'Channel Firing', was written in late 1914, after the initial euphoria, at a point when it was clear that the war in Europe would not be quickly won, and our boys would not be back by Christmas. The war, God help us, might even be lost, and with it Old England, forever. The jackboot would goose-step on consecrated English soil.

The sound of the nearby war wakes the corpses no longer resting in peace in their Wessex graveyard (Hardy had a strong line in ghosts). Corpses and war make good company. But those gun batteries, fortifying the coast and the Channel, which, thank God, disconnects us from Europe, will defend England. They will, with every volley, preserve Old England – the England that stretches back in time as far as Stonehenge. Every thoughtful Brexiteer's heart will throb harder, reading and rereading this strange but paramountly England-loving poem. It is a cadaver who speaks, buried in peacetime and woken by the ruckus of war:

> That night your great guns, unawares,
> Shook all our coffins as we lay,
> And broke the chancel window-squares,
> We thought it was the Judgment-day
>
> And sat upright. While drearisome
> Arose the howl of wakened hounds:
> The mouse let fall the altar-crumb,
> The worms drew back into the mounds,
>
> The glebe cow drooled. Till God called, 'No;
> It's gunnery practice out at sea
> Just as before you went below;
> The world is as it used to be:
>
> 'All nations striving strong to make
> Red war yet redder. Mad as hatters

They do no more for Christés sake
Than you who are helpless in such matters.

'That this is not the judgment-hour
For some of them's a blessed thing,
For if it were they'd have to scour
Hell's floor for so much threatening . . .

'Ha, ha. It will be warmer when
I blow the trumpet (if indeed
I ever do; for you are men,
And rest eternal sorely need).'

So down we lay again. 'I wonder,
Will the world ever saner be,'
Said one, 'than when He sent us under
In our indifferent century!'

And many a skeleton shook his head.
'Instead of preaching forty year,'
My neighbour Parson Thirdly said,
'I wish I had stuck to pipes and beer.'

Again the guns disturbed the hour,
Roaring their readiness to avenge,
As far inland as Stourton Tower,
And Camelot, and starlit Stonehenge.

'Starlit Stonehenge' is, for my money, the most evocative two-word image in English poetry.

DNB/OED

There are two vast compilations that, for the purpose of literary guidance, every Brexiteer should have on his or her bookshelf, wood or electronic: the OED (*Oxford English Dictionary*) and the DNB (*Dictionary of National Biography*).[67] With their titles' stress on 'English' and 'National', both resources embody the confidence of the Victorian England/Britain in which they were launched – a confidence sadly diminished in the late twentieth century. Did space permit, one could add to the list of these two Brexit companion volumes the tenth (1903) edition of the *Encyclopædia Britannica*, the Fowler brothers' *Modern English Usage* and Paul Harvey's *Oxford Companion to English Literature*.

The oldest English publisher (there is some little bickering with Cambridge on the matter) OUP (Oxford University Press) was founded nearly half a millennium ago on the rubble of Henry VIII's 'reformed' ecclesiastical structures, which became Oxbridge (ever wonder why the students are gowned?). The important point about the OED is that it is historical: in most cases it assumes a long Englishness behind every English word.[68] It's not archaeological, it's 'organic'. It's a beautiful conceit. The OED does not 'define' (as *Larousse* does); it anatomizes living verbal tissue.

No one mind can 'know' the English language in its entirety. Might as well try to memorize all the stars in the sky. It's a constant, unending stream of definition and discovery. The oed has traditionally employed 'slips' – usage found and sent in by scores, sometimes hundreds, of (unpaid, unacknowledged) readers who have 'come across' something interesting. One feels a national collectivity behind every entry. There is no other book enterprise quite like it.

The OED is constantly updating itself, as we see from the (still short, soon to be much longer) entry on the word (of course that word) 'Brexit':

Pronunciation: Brit. /ˈbrɛksɪt/, /ˈbrɛgzɪt/, u.s. / ˈbrɛgzət/, /ˈbrɛksət/
Forms: 20– **Brexit**, 20– **Brixit** (*rare*).
Origin: Formed within English, by compounding.
Etymons: BRITISH *adj.*, EXIT *n.*
Etymology: < *Br-* (in BRITISH *adj.*) and EXIT *n.*, after GREXIT *n.*

The (proposed) withdrawal of the UK from the EU, and the political process associated with it.

Sometimes used specifically with reference to the referendum held in the UK on 23 June 2016, in which a majority of voters favoured withdrawal from the EU.

2012 P. Wilding in *BlogActiv.eu* (Blog) 15 May (**oed** Archive) (*title*). Stumbling towards the Brexit: Britain, a referendum and an ever-closer reckoning.

2012 *Christian Sci. Monitor* (Nexis) 10 Oct. Why would the EU consider special economic and trading privileges for Britain after its 'Brexit'?

2014 *Financial Times* (Electronic ed.) 19 Aug. 16. In many cases, the u.s. banks are as worried about the Eurozone's impending banking union as they are about Brexit.

2016 *Globe & Mail* (Toronto) (Nexis) 12 July. Ms. May insisted that whatever her views, the country had spoken. 'Brexit means Brexit and we're going to make a success of it. There will be no attempts to remain inside the EU,' she said.

2016 *Daily Mirror* (Nexis) 13 Oct. 14. A soft Brexit would see us maintain access to the single market and the customs union and accept some EU rules. A hard Brexit would see us quit the single market and the customs union in return for control of our borders.

The important point about the other essential set of books, the dnb, is that it surveys, as far back as biography can look, only personages who are British. Also predominantly – until very modern times – male and English.[69]

Both enterprises came into the care of OUP, like foundlings left on the doorstep of the Clarendon Building. The oed was the brainchild of the Philological Society in the second half of the nineteenth century. The first general editor, Herbert Coleridge, was a grandson of the poet (who would have loved the enterprise). The driving force of the dictionary before it became an OUP possession was the philologist Frederick Furnivall, who was, as Peter Sutcliffe describes him in his chatty history of OUP,

a man of turbulent character, part clown, part scholar, a charlatan of fanatical integrity . . . living proof of the foolhardiness of the whole enterprise. Teetotal, non-smoking, vegetarian, over-exercised, he was also an agnostic and an anti-sabbatarian, who married a lady's-maid and compounded the offence by leaving her.[70]

Furnivall was aided by Henry Sweet – George Bernard Shaw's Professor Henry Higgins in *Pygmalion* – who was also high in the league of great English eccentrics. My favourite anecdote about the OED is that those working on it, day and night, assembled the elephant ledgers into a bomb shelter (within which they continued working) when the air-raid sirens sounded in Oxford during the Second World War.

The OED was inherited by OUP from the Philological Society, for whom it was, they discovered, too large a job, in 1879. The dnb was likewise inherited by OUP in 1917, the worst year of the war – a moment when England, and what it stood for, was imperilled. The venture had been begun in 1882 by the publisher George Smith, the patron of virtually every great literary figure of the high Victorian period, from Charlotte Brontë to Thackeray, via Eliot and Browning (only Dickens slipped his net). Smith's DNB was taken charge of by Leslie Stephen, man of letters and father of Virginia Woolf.

The dnb was, said one OUP grandee, a 'damnosa heriditas', a damnable bequest. But the Press took it on and raised the venture from mere biographical dictionary to great national institution. Like the OED, the DNB is a 'living organism', the incarnation of Englishness as it evolves, through the English people. It is not, although all its entries are of the dead, a mere bundle of obituaries or a 'Who was Who'. Underneath it all is the search for what makes England England and England great.

It is appropriate to demonstrate the dnb here with Simon Heffer's entry on Enoch Powell, one of those rare politicians whose influence (for good or ill) after death has been greater than while he lived. Particularly on Brexit. The entry is massive in length; extracted here is Heffer's account of the crucial episode in Powell's career – his defiant break with the Conservative Party, bluntly the post-Rivers of Blood imbroglio (see 'Rivers of Blood Wash over Our Green and Pleasant Land' above). Heffer, who has written an OED-dependent manual on 'good' English usage, is, like Powell, a master of trenchant prose:

THE BIRMINGHAM SPEECH

Since the mid-1950s, Powell had, when in government, argued on departmental committees that mass immigration was having a damaging effect on certain parts of the country where immigrants tended to settle ...

In the spring of 1968, at a time when his relations with Heath and many of his colleagues were strained in any case, Powell expressed dissatisfaction with his party's relatively conciliatory position on the Race Relations Bill, which was then going through parliament. He felt that the Conservative leaders, few of whom sat as he did for constituencies with large immigrant populations, simply did not understand the unhappiness of many people at what was being done to their communities without their having been consulted ... [Then] on 20 April 1968 Powell made a speech at the Midland Hotel, Birmingham, about immigration. This speech thereafter defined his place in British political culture. He told the story of a little old lady, the last white woman in her street, who was taunted by immigrants and had excrement pushed through her letterbox. Sensing the chorus of execration that was about to break over him, he said that he had no right to remain silent when things such as this were happening to his electors. He predicted that, unless something was done to stop mass immigration, there would be a breakdown in public order. 'Like the Roman,' he told his audience, quoting Virgil, 'I seem to see the River Tiber foaming with much blood' (Powell, *Freedom and Reality*, 1969, 213–19).

Heath, angry at being caught unawares by the speech, decided that it was racist in tone, and sacked Powell the next day ... A month after his speech Gallup found that

74 per cent of people agreed with Powell, 15 per cent disagreed, and 11 per cent did not know (Gallup, 1026).

There was staunch – rabid it was called – support for Powell, which at its extreme manifested in street agitation:

> He received over 100,000 letters in the weeks after his speech, only a small proportion of which disagreed with him. Heath, by contrast, had the obloquy of his party's grass roots heaped upon him. Trade unionists, to the embarrassment of the Labour leadership, marched to the Commons from the London docks and the Smithfield meat market in support of Powell. Although the furore was hard on Powell and particularly upon his wife and two daughters, he came to terms with his sudden celebrity, and sought to take advantage of the freedom his new position on the backbenches allowed him.
>
> 'I felt like a man walking down a street who is hit on the head by a tile falling from a roof ... I saw it immediately that I would never hold office again; and I determined to make the best use I could of my circumstances.' (*The Independent*, 9 Feb 1998)

The little old lady, Heffer records, has never been found. It is a finely judicious description of the moment when Powell's flawed greatness let him, and his less inflammatory ideas, down. To repeat his best-known aphorism: 'All political lives, unless they are cut off in midstream at a happy juncture, end in failure, because that is the nature of politics and of human affairs.' His own failure was precipitate after one night in 1968.

Land of Hope and Glory

Were some unusually enterprising pollster to take an exit poll among those spilling out of the Albert Hall after the Last Night of the Proms, it is odds-on that there would be a rock-solid vote for Brexit. For the millions merely watching the event on TV, it is not clear whether what they are seeing on their screens is a concert or a chaotic English version of a Nuremberg rally with music. Not even the malign genius of Leni Riefenstahl, however, could make the Last Night look organized. The musical programme of this orgy of pent-up, amp II nationalism climaxes with 'Land of Hope and Glory', with the audience joining in raucously. (Quite possibly, they have warmed up with 'Jerusalem'; see 'Brexit's Green and Pleasant Land' above.)

The words of the poem 'Land of Hope and Glory' express a frank yearning in the past for English global expansion. As things are now, the song, as sung at the Proms, represents nostalgia for a lost empire whose idea the audience does not ever want to let go of. Dream on. Does UKIP, in its heart, want global conquest, Empire regained? Does it want to make England 'conquer' – and become 'mightier yet' – or does Brexit merely want to keep 'our' borders as tight as a side drum? Does it idealize a 'Little England' getting smaller by the decade until all its 'mighty' force is compressed into something as tiny as an atom, insignificant but mightily explosive?

In the 1960s a feeble attempt to suppress the Last Night's 'Hope and Glory' audience orgy was overwhelmingly protested down.[71] The version of the song bellowed in the Albert Hall – a building named after a German prince who married an Anglo-Germanic monarch – was put together by the composer Edward Elgar and the dandy *littérateur* A. C. Benson a few months after Queen Victoria's death. Her spirit, it was determined, should live on, and for a few years it did.

Given the Teutonic connection of the British Royal Family, it might have been as appropriate to sing 'Deutschland, Deutschland über Alles'. But Edward VII loved Elgar's ultra-English 'Pomp and Circumstance' marches and commissioned a version of one of them for his coronation, in 1902. 'Land of Hope and Glory' was the result, along with a knighthood for the composer. The version sung at the Proms is simpler, but the sentiment is the same as that rung to the rafters in Westminster Abbey, for Victoria's royal successor, in 1902:

> *Solo*
> Dear Land of Hope, thy hope is crowned,
> God make thee mightier yet!
> On Sov'ran brows, beloved, renowned,
> Once more thy crown is set.
> Thine equal laws, by Freedom gained,
> Have ruled thee well and long;
> By Freedom gained, by Truth maintained,
> Thine Empire shall be strong.

> *Chorus*
> Land of Hope and Glory, Mother of the Free,
> How shall we extol thee, who are born of thee?
> Wider still and wider shall thy bounds be set;
> God, who made thee mighty, make thee mightier yet,
> God, who made thee mighty, make thee mightier yet.

> *Solo*
> Thy fame is ancient as the days,
> As Ocean large and wide:
> A pride that dares, and heeds not praise,

A stern and silent pride;
Not that false joy that dreams content
With what our sires have won;
The blood a hero sire hath spent
Still nerves a hero son.

Mightier yet, in 2018? Our 'sires'? What century is this song living in?

The composition of the poem coincided, meaningfully, with the publication of Cecil Rhodes's preposterous last will and testament, and its dedication to a wholly global British Empire, including the USA (recolonized) and China.

Benson, a rather sad man and discreetly homosexual in his years as a high don at Cambridge, may have yearned for a little more 'freedom' to be granted his private life. Like many gay men in that brutal time, he sported a thick, 'manly' moustache lest anyone suspect a hint of Oscarism. The trial of Wilde did wonders for the Harris tweed and golf-club industries. In one of his stranger utterances, Nigel Farage suggested that privately held homophobia is bearably widespread – in the over-seventies. One of the comforts of modern retirement *durée*, presumably.

While we're on the subject of sex, Edward Elgar in our regenerate day might well have joined Rolf Harris in some open prison and composed an anthem for the didgeridoo. There are accounts that he was in the habit of insisting that his female choir members wear blue knickers and checking Elgarian uniformity with his walking stick. Finding a transgressor, he is reported to have snorted, 'Well, you're no Virgin Mary' (few women, to be theological, are – one only in recorded history).[72]

Orwell: Quarter-French, Wholly English[73]

In one of his many meditations on Englishness, 'England your England', George Orwell identified 'gentleness' as the country's salient characteristic. He was writing, as he said, while civilized men in German bombers overhead were trying ungently to kill him. His remarks, and his diagnosis of this peculiarly English quality, could well be adopted as the UKIP manifesto:

> One cannot see the modern world as it is unless one recognizes the overwhelming strength of patriotism, national loyalty. In certain circumstances it can break down, at certain levels of civilization it does not exist, but as a *positive* force there is nothing to set beside it. Christianity and international Socialism are as weak as straw in comparison with it. Hitler and Mussolini rose to power in their own countries very largely because they could grasp this fact and their opponents could not.
>
> Also, one must admit that the divisions between nation and nation are founded on real differences of outlook. Till recently it was thought proper to pretend that all human beings are very much alike, but in fact anyone able to use his eyes knows that the average of human behaviour differs enormously from country to country. Things that could happen in one country could not happen in another. Hitler's June purge, for instance, could not have happened in England. And, as western peoples go, the English are very highly differentiated. There is a sort of backhanded admission of this in the dislike which nearly all foreigners feel for our national way of life. Few Europeans can endure living in England, and even Americans often feel more at home in Europe.

When you come back to England from any foreign country, you have immediately the sensation of breathing a different air. Even in the firſt few minutes dozens of small things conspire to give you this feeling. The beer is bitterer, the coins are heavier, the grass is greener, the advertisements are more blatant. The crowds in the big towns, with their mild knobby faces, their bad teeth and gentle manners, are different from a European crowd. Then the vaſtness of England swallows you up, and you lose for a while your feeling that the whole nation has a single identifiable charaĉter. Are there really such things as nations? Are we not forty-six million individuals, all different? And the diversity of it, the chaos! The clatter of clogs in the Lancashire mill towns, the to-and-fro of the lorries on the Great North Road, the queues outside the Labour Exchanges, the rattle of pin-tables in the Soho pubs, the old maids biking to Holy Communion through the miſts of the autumn morning – all these are not only fragments, but *charaĉteriſtic* fragments, of the English scene. How can one make a pattern out of this muddle?

But talk to foreigners, read foreign books or news-papers, and you are brought back to the same thought. Yes, there *is* something diſtinĉtive and recognizable in English civilization. It is a culture as individual as that of Spain. It is somehow bound up with solid breakfaſts and gloomy Sundays, smoky towns and winding roads, green fields and red pillar-boxes. It has a flavour of its own. Moreover it is continuous, it ſtretches into the future and the paſt, there is something in it that persiſts, as in a living creature. What can the England of 1940 have in common with the England of 1840? But then, what have you in common with the child of five whose photograph your mother keeps on the mantelpiece? Nothing, except that you happen to be the same person.

And above all, it is *your* civilization, it is *you*. However much you hate it or laugh at it, you will never be happy away from it for any length of time. [Orwell's emphasis]

The Trollopian red pillar box is a typically Orwellian touch, in this beautifully observed portrait of England – a portrait all the sharper since, at that moment, during the Blitz of 1941, it was not at all certain that England would survive.

Orwell's nightmare, as he slowly suffocated to death from tuberculosis in University College London's hospital in late 1949, was that this peculiar England, having survived the war, was becoming, under Attlee's 'Socialism', what? 'Airstrip One'; with the glorious English language, bundled in those ever-growing volumes of the oed, becoming so skeletal as not to be language at all. A few hundred words of 'newspeak' from which all significant thought had been bleached out. Doubleplus bad.

In the above encomium to England, the word that resonates is 'gentle', and I think it has a consonance with Jane Austen's 'English comfort' in *Emma*, discussed above. There is no question, as has been said, how she would have voted – her cross would have joined that of the majority in Hampshire. And Orwell? How would he have voted? His mother being half-French, he might have been expected to straddle the fence. He loved England, as he makes clear above, but hated the British Empire, as he makes clear in his first novel, *Burmese Days* (1934). In the booth he would have considered carefully, I think, but, with a muttered 'my country right or wrong', and many second thoughts, he would have gone, at the critical moment and with a wavering pencil, for Leave.

Rhodes Must Fall. Kipling Must Go. Buchan Goes On and On

O ne of the interesting aspects of the referendum for future historians will be its having mapped out what 'English-ness 2017' was, and, more interestingly, UKIP's essential quarrel with what 2017 England had become. For example, bubbling away in the newly expanded and 'democratized' university sector was the National Union of Students and its leaders, posing their question of the day: 'Why is my curriculum so white?' Brexit's whiteness was a damnably sore point for these radicals.

At the other extreme, the English Defence League (EDL) and Britain First were trying to get their Dr Martens in at the door, or through it. They demonstrated alongside Farage, whom they anointed (to his utter disgust) as their patriot saint and guru, and advertised him, standing in front of a proudly blowing Union Jack, with the motto 'Join Nigel Farage' (i.e. get in step with the EDL). The referendum was the best publicity these far-right groups got until, in November 2017, the 45th President of the United States, Donald Trump, retweeted approvingly three of their anti-Islamic propaganda videos.

As regards student radicals, the conflict boiled over with the 'Rhodes Must Fall' campaign. Cecil Rhodes's rise to a prime position among the world's potentates began at Oriel College, Oxford. He went on to enrich himself with diamonds dug by black indentured hands from the South African soil, and founded the firm De Beers. By the end of the nineteenth century 90 per cent of the world's new diamonds passed through De Beers, leaving the financial residue to the African countries in whose ground they had been stored for millennia. In the idiom of the day, De Beers 'cornered' – and still dominates – the market, with Cecil Rhodes, both alive and dead, at its apex. A diamond is forever, as the advertisement puts it. So, it would seem, is De Beers.

Historically, Rhodes is regarded as the father of apartheid. As implemented by Hendrik Verwoerd in the 1950s and 1960s, it took as its founding belief 'never the twain shall meet' ('twain' being a matter of pigment). That phrase originates in Rudyard Kipling's 'Ballad of East and West': 'Oh, East is East and West is West, and never the twain shall meet,/ Till Earth and Sky stand presently at God's great Judgment Seat.' Kipling was intimate with Rhodes, both personally and intellectually. On occasions when fine words were required to cover his deeds, Rhodes would ask Kipling to write something for him. Kipling often enough obliged, but usually with little subversions. He was not a court poet.

Rhodes was committed to eternal British domination of the African countries that had made him fabulously rich, even if it cost a large spillage of Tommy Atkins's blood, as it did in the Boer Wars.[74] Unluckily, he died of a heart attack aged a mere 49 in November 1902, a few weeks before the Boer collapse. Statues in his memory sprang up, like dragon's teeth, all over South Africa.

Kipling was by Rhodes's bed during his last illness, and attended the great man's funeral, walking prominently in the cortège. He wrote a panegyric that he himself read aloud as the coffin was lowered into the African soil:

> 'The Burial'
> (*C. J. Rhodes, buried in the Matoppos, April 10, 1902*)
>
> When that great Kings return to clay,
>   Or Emperors in their pride,

Grief of a day shall fill a day,
    Because its creature died.
But we – we reckon not with those
    Whom the mere Fates ordain,
This Power that wrought on us and goes
    Back to the Power again.

Dreamer devout, by vision led
    Beyond our guess or reach,
The travail of his spirit bred
    Cities in place of speech.
So huge the all-mastering thought that drove –
    So brief the term allowed –
Nations, not words, he linked to prove
    His faith before the crowd.

It is his will that he look forth
    Across the world he won –
The granite of the ancient North –
    Great spaces washed with sun.
There shall he patient take his seat
    (As when the Death he dared),
And there await a people's feet
    In the paths that he prepared.

There, till the vision he foresaw
    Splendid and whole arise,
And unimagined Empires draw
    To council 'neath his skies,
The immense and brooding Spirit still
    Shall quicken and control.
Living he was the land, and dead,
    His soul shall be her soul!

There is a subtext to the poem. Rhodes had been worried, in his later years, about Kipling's evident scepticism about the dreamer devout (Rhodes himself) and his vision of global Anglo-Saxon racial supremacy. Kipling was not quite sure about that future historical outcome, or whether he approved it. Nonetheless, 'The Burial' was cablegrammed to *The Times* and *New York Times*, which published it within hours. Few readers would have pondered subtextual complexities. Rhodes was a great man and Kipling a great poet; the twain had met.

Rhodes's tentacles around vast expanses of Africa ('the land') were memorialized in the territories named Northern Rhodesia and Southern Rhodesia. No other country in recorded history has borne a colonist's name. The African tributes remained so named until 'independence' in the 1960s, when they became Zambia and Zimbabwe respectively. The renaming was accompanied by much pulling down of public statuary – primarily Rhodes's and Queen Victoria's statues. Africa was strenuously de-Rhodesing itself.

Rhodes himself had been terrified by that awful prospect during his last months on earth. Would he be an Ozymandias, forgotten under the dust of history, his name unremembered, even obliterated – the tyrant's deathbed nightmare (it's good to recall that Saddam Hussein lived to see his statue torn down and defiled)? By careful disposition of his colossal wealth, Rhodes made vigorous efforts to forestall such a catastrophe and to continue, after his death, his work for Anglo-Saxon supremacy, by a kind of Rhodesian Masonic secret society, if necessary. This end was stated explicitly in his will. His vast treasure would be dedicated, as he had specified earlier, to

> the establishment, promotion and development of a
> Secret Society, the true aim and object whereof shall be
> for the extension of British rule throughout the world,

the perfecting of a system of emigration from the United Kingdom, and of colonisation by British subjects of all lands where the means of livelihood are attainable by energy, labour and enterprise, and especially the occupation by British settlers of the entire Continent of Africa, the Holy Land, the Valley of the Euphrates, the Islands of Cyprus and Candia, the whole of South America, the Islands of the Pacific not heretofore possessed by Great Britain, the whole of the Malay Archipelago, the seaboard of China and Japan.

The 'entire Continent'? 'Secret Society'?

Rhodes left a munificent bequest to his college, along with other benefactions to the Oxford he loved. Unsurprisingly, the Dreaming Spires loved him. Oriel erected a statue in its patron's honour, dominating the college facade: I own this place, the statue seems to declare.

Posthumously trundling his chariot of fire across the globe, Rhodes left the University of Oxford a large sum for the establishment of a 'Rhodes' scholarship programme designed to aid students (overwhelmingly American) to study at 'his' university. The fellowship's founding principle was that it would advance the interest of Anglo-Saxon (British and American) racial stock. Other racial stock was of no matter. The programme was run by Rhodes House, an Oxford college in all but name.

The terms under which Rhodes founded his scholars' programme were uncompromising. It was directed to 'young [male] colonists' possessed of the necessary moral fibre and leadership qualities to work for 'the furtherance of the British Empire, for the bringing of the whole uncivilised world under British rule, for the recovery of the United States, for the making the Anglo-Saxon race but one Empire'. The repossession (recolonization) of the United States was a daring touch. In the event, WASP(ish) cultural domination would have to do. It lasted in broad terms until 20 January 2009, when an African American took over the White House.

Over the years Rhodes's grand projects were cut back. In recent years the fellowship was opened up to women and to what would, in Rhodes's view, have been 'lesser races'. In other words, it was turned upside down. Black people were, however, excluded until 1991, before which their admittance was conceived a contradiction too far. The furtherance of the British Empire is not mentioned in the 2017 Rhodes Scholar prospectus.

The Oxford 'Rhodes Must Fall' campaign landed some heavy punches, as expressed in its opening petition:

> As long as the statue remains, Oriel College and Oxford University continue to tacitly identify with Rhodes's values, and to maintain a toxic culture of domination and oppression. This statue is an open glorification of the racist and bloody project of British colonialism. An architect of apartheid in Southern Africa, Rhodes is the same apartheid colonialist who said: 'I prefer land to niggers . . . the natives are like children. They are just emerging from barbarism . . . one should kill as many niggers as possible'.

He didn't, as it happens, quite say that.[75] But things were reaching a point where precise 'truth' as opposed to 'fake truth' didn't really come into it. And what Rhodes actually believed is proclaimed, plainly enough, in his 'Confession of Faith' of 1877:

> I contend that we [THE ENGLISH] are the finest race in the world and that the more of the world we inhabit the better it is for the human race. Just fancy those parts that are at present inhabited by the most despicable

specimens of human beings what an alteration there would be if they were brought under Anglo-Saxon influence, look again at the extra employment a new country added to our dominions gives . . . Why should we not form a secret society with but one object the furtherance of the British Empire and the bringing of the whole uncivilised world under British rule for the recovery of the United States for the making the Anglo-Saxon race but one Empire. What a dream, but yet it is probable, it is possible.

The dream had somewhat lost its lustre in 2016. And you could have built a pyramid, or a slag heap, from the rubble of felled statues of Cecil John Rhodes in decolonized Africa.

The British man in the street – the average UKIP supporter, one can hazard – didn't know Cecil Rhodes from a Greek island. The 'Rhodes Must Fall' campaign originated not in Oxford but on the campus of the University of Cape Town, in March 2015. The university boasted a truly imperial statue of Rhodes, whose principal home had been in Cape Town. He had, as with Oriel, been generous to the South African university. Tearing down the statue – daubed with human shit, by way of opening shot – was publicized as a Cromwellian act of moral purification. Within weeks the wrecking ball and diggers did their decolonizing obsequies. Rhodes duly fell. Another 'Burial', this time with no Kipling to lament it. Oxford students mobilized round a follow-up, web-fuelled campaign to smash, or at least remove, the statue of Rhodes ornamenting Oriel College. Pigeons had already done their work on the shit.

Elsewhere in Oxford, the Rhodes Scholars programme had, by 2016, relaxed its founding racist imperatives. The campaign was led by the very un-Anglo-Saxon Rhodes Scholar Ntokozo Qwabe, a South African studying law. He was black, dissident and manifestly very clever. Whatever pittance dribbled back to him as a Rhodes Scholar he deemed irrelevant, in the face of what Rhodes had taken from his country. Qwabe felt not the slightest embarrassment at biting the hand that fed him. A million Rhodes scholars, by his reckoning, would not level the amount Rhodes had stripped from the soil of his country.

'Rhodes Must Fall' was small-time in itself. It was seen as students getting above themselves, as they invariably do before they encounter the 'real world' outside their ivory towers. But the campaign was much bruited and attacked in the populist press (the *Mail*, *Express* and *Sun*). It *meant* something. No one quite dared express it, but this was where the EU's open door to immigration (free movement of people) would lead. Tearing down all that had made Britain Britain.[76]

For Oriel, it was the biggest thing since John Henry Newman (an Oriel man) and his 'Tracts for the Times' tore Oxford apart, those 'times' being the 1840s. Headlines thundered, Oriel quivered fearfully, and the nation took an ominous interest in a minor Oxbridge squabble. After painful wavering, the college eventually resisted. The Rhodes statue would remain for pigeons to filth up, but token amends would be made. An inculpating plaque, perhaps.

Oriel's age-withered arm was strengthened by a survey that revealed, unsurprisingly, that if there were one thing the un-gowned 'people', who make up the mass of the UK voting population, did not want, it was toffee-nosed undergraduates with names they couldn't spell telling them that they must feel guilty about being British because of what their ancestors had done in far-off places in times long gone by. A YouGov survey in January 2016 'found that 59% of [Oxford] respondents thought the statue of Cecil Rhodes on Oriel's High Street facade should *not* be taken down'. It was later revealed to be not far off the Leave majority in the referendum. If there was one thing the

British were not ashamed about, it was the British Empire. The survey further reported:

> In response to the related topic of the British Empire, the survey highlighted surprising deviations from what are perceived to be the prevailing attitudes at Oxford University. 43% voted that the British Empire was 'generally speaking' a good thing though a partisan breakdown offered some further points of interest. While only 28% of those who voted Labour at the last election designated the Empire 'a good thing', the corresponding figures for the Liberal Democrats, Conservatives and UKIP were 42%, 55% and 63% respectively.

Note that thumping UKIP figure. The 'Rhodes Must Fall' campaign probably cost the Remain campaign crucial votes in what would prove on the night to be a close fight. And Rhodes did not fall – at least not in England. His statue stands, spattered by pigeon droppings, but inviolate.

Kipling Again

R udyard Kipling was Rhodes's favourite poet and a close friend. He is also, one might hazard, the laureate of UKIP. There is to be found on YouTube Nigel Farage's rousing recitation of the poem 'If'.[77] The poem has anthemic status in the movement, along with 'Land of Hope and Glory' and 'Jerusalem'. Farage – against all the odds and defying every 'if' obstructing him – got his movement off the ground, kept it going and raised it to triumph in June 2016. 'You all laughed,' he said in his victory speech to the European Parliament, where he is the bolshiest of MEPs; 'you're not laughing now.' Sweet words in his mouth.[78]

Kipling's poem begins: 'If you can keep your head when all about you/ Are losing theirs and blaming it on you.' Through the long years of Europhile darkness, under Farage's tutelage, the Party indeed kept its head – with an occasional blowing of its top. The poem ends: 'Yours is the Earth and everything that's in it,/ And – which is more – you'll be a Man, my son!' UKIP's manhood came on 24 June 2016. They had killed their lion. England and its future were theirs.

Kipling was the first English-language writer to win the Nobel Prize in Literature, in 1907. Ten years earlier, instead of the etiolated poet laureate of the time, Alfred Austin, Kipling was recruited to write the poem he called 'Recessional', for Victoria's Diamond Jubilee. There are always two or three Kiplings tussling inconclusively in his serious efforts, and this is an oddly conflicted composition. Here the poet foresees the decline and fall of the empire he has specifically been charged to jubilate, in diamonds (the Rhodesian stone):

> God of our fathers, known of old,
> > Lord of our far-flung battle line,
> Beneath whose awful hand we hold
> > Dominion over palm and pine –
> Lord God of Hosts, be with us yet,
> Lest we forget – lest we forget!
> The tumult and the shouting dies;
> > The Captains and the Kings depart:
> Still stands Thine ancient sacrifice,
> > An humble and a contrite heart.
> Lord God of Hosts, be with us yet,
> Lest we forget – lest we forget!
>
> Far-called our navies melt away;
> > On dune and headland sinks the fire:

Lo, all our pomp of yesterday
    Is one with Nineveh and Tyre!
Judge of the Nations, spare us yet,
Lest we forget – lest we forget!

If, drunk with sight of power, we loose
    Wild tongues that have not Thee in awe,
Such boastings as the Gentiles use,
    Or lesser breeds without the Law –
Lord God of Hosts, be with us yet,
Lest we forget – lest we forget!

For heathen heart that puts her trust
    In reeking tube and iron shard,
All valiant dust that builds on dust,
    And guarding calls not Thee to guard,
For frantic boast and foolish word –
Thy Mercy on Thy People, Lord!

'Our navies melt away'! Somewhere beyond the veil, Kipling must be congratulating himself on his percipience.

At the same period, and in the same wobbly frame of mind, Kipling wrote a lament called 'The White Man's Burden' (1899). The subject is world leadership that must now, since the British Empire is visibly declining, be passed on to the other great Anglo-Saxon 'race', the United States. That alliance, as his will testifies, Rhodes thought essential to the future of the planet.

The USA was at the time engaged in the Philippines war, a bloody colonial episode that American history does not like to dwell on. Casualties were appalling: some 4,000 American soldiers died, and as many as a million Filipino combatants and civilians. Harsh American reprisals against the people of the Philippines are recorded.

How can England's 'National Curriculum' include 'If' and blank out 'The White Man's Burden'? Can one, to pursue the question, imagine Nigel Farage feelingly reciting 'The White Man's Burden' as he does 'If' on YouTube (14,000 hits and rising)? To read the poem answers the question:

> Take up the White Man's burden –
> Send forth the beſt ye breed –
> Go bind your sons to exile
> To serve your captives' need;
> To wait in heavy harness
> On fluttered folk and wild –
> Your new-caught sullen peoples,
> Half devil and half child.

One needn't quote the whole thing. There's more than enough in the first stanza.

Nigel Farage's Favourite Novel

Answering a survey question in 2015, Nigel Farage nominated as his favourite work of prose fiction John Buchan's *The Thirty-nine Steps* (1915).[79] 'Thoroughly predictable,' commented *The Guardian*, sourly.

Buchan's novel is a story about saving England from wicked Europe. It has been adapted into classic cinema (by Hitchcock, notably) and successful TV versions. A dramatic version is running in the West End as I write.

The British reading public has always loved Buchan's 'shilling shocker', as its author deprecatingly called it. It was conceived at a critical moment in Britain's involvement with Europe. As the First World War broke out in September 1914

Buchan, in his late thirties – a high-flyer in whatever he chose to turn his hand to – was recovering from a duodenal ulcer, the occupational hazard of high-flyers. To entertain himself and others, he resolved to throw off a rattling yarn. On the side it would be a work that would 'do his bit' for the war effort, since he was too old and now medically too crocked to fight.

Buchan modelled his plot on Erskine Childers's bestselling spy story *The Riddle of the Sands* (1903), which is subtitled *A Record of Secret Service Recently Achieved* (the actual Secret Service government agency did not, of course, yet exist, but is forecast). The story is written in pseudo-documentary style with accompanying maps. The chronicle that forms Childers's narrative is dated '1903', and the hero-narrator is Carruthers of the FO. He describes himself, with saving facetiousness, as 'a young man of condition and fashion, who knows the right people, belongs to the right clubs, has a safe, possibly a brilliant, future in the Foreign Office'.

Just at that moment, the young man of condition and fashion is finding London tedious. It is late summer. The West End bores him and he longs for the four bracing winds of the seas and a little light relief from 'the dismal but dignified routine of office, club and chambers'. The 'big picture' is sketched in the background: Germany is secretly arming itself ('she grows, and strengthens, and waits').

Carruthers and his old college pal Arthur H. Davies go off sailing on the yacht *Dulcibella* in the sandbar-bedevilled Baltic waters. There, to their patriotic alarm, the young men stumble across Germany's plans for the invasion of England. There is much accompanying descriptive detail of ropes, tackle and canvas. On their return, the Admiralty is informed. The necessary precautions must and will be taken against the wily Hun.

Childers's novel – simplistic as it is – can plausibly be credited with a number of achievements. The first is that it pioneered a genre: the spy/secret agent docu-novel. Second, it usefully (from the authorities' point of view) whipped up anti-German sentiment in the long run-up to the First World War. Third, it inspired the creation of a number of naval bases on the North Sea coast, aimed to increase British readiness for any invasion from that direction. Winston Churchill, as First Lord of the Admiralty, was a staunch admirer of *The Riddle of the Sands*. So, I would guess, is Nigel Farage, if he has come across it. That line 'she [Germany] grows, and strengthens, and waits' is highly UKIP appropriate.

Buchan's story opens in May 1914, the last summer of Olde England. It's the summer that Philip Larkin memorializes in his elegiac poem 'MCMXIV' (see 'Philip Larkin: The Greatest English Poet of Our Time' below). *The Thirty-nine Steps* reached publication belatedly in 1915, as it began to dawn on the nation that the war was going to be a long haul – and, horrible thought, that England might lose. The fact that England had a German king (cousin to the Kaiser) was no consolation.

Buchan's hero, Richard Hannay, is an old (South) Africa hand, a Boer War veteran enriched by gold-mining. He is the kind of man Rhodes would have seen as the salt of the earth; that is, a bit like himself.[80] English students in AD 2017 would have readily done a pigeon-shit job on Hannay's statue, too. Diamonds, gold – what else could the English colonials steal? Hannay, having signed up and had a good (First World) war, is the lead character in a succession of Buchan's novels, in which he invariably saves England, in one way or another, from dastardly Johnny Foreigner. In that respect he is up there with James Bond (who owes much to Hannay) in the pantheon of English literary heroism.

Buchan's fiction is permeated with racism that has not lasted well, and that is necessarily bleached from modern stage, film and TV adaptations. In *The Thirty-nine Steps*, for example, there has been fierce dispute about an anti-Semitic outburst by one of the minor characters, Scudder, who affects to know all the shady things that are going on behind the scenes in the world. To quote one of Scudder's less offensive lines, 'The Jew is everywhere, but you have to go far down the backstairs to find him.'

The jury is still out, and forever will be, one guesses, on where Buchan stood. I tend to acquit him. More interesting, in view of the present state of affairs, is Buchan's view of race globally. It is expressed most articulately (he was never at a loss for eloquence) in his earlier novel of ideas, *A Lodge in the Wilderness* (1906), a work which reads at times like a prose version of Kipling's 'The White Man's Burden'.

Thinkers, nine men and nine women, have gathered for a conference called at a lodge in the Kenyan highlands by a multi-millionaire, Francis Carey, enriched by African colonial exploitation. Half the continent is 'his'. Carey is manifestly Buchan's obituary portrait of Rhodes. The topic under discussion among this seminar of the great is 'Empire'. By way of recreation there is a lion hunt. What else? It's a kind of Bilderberg before Bilderberg. England has just won the Boer War, putting its imperial heel forever on the richest country in the continent of Africa.

One discussant comes out with a declaration that is *echt* Buchan. No claptrap is necessary, he ('Mr Wakefield') decrees:

'For Heaven's sake let us keep out of mysticism,' broke in Mr Wakefield, who detested Lord Appin's metaphysics. 'I define Imperialism as the closer organic connection under one Crown of a number of autonomous nations of the same blood, who can spare something of their vitality for the administration of vast tracts inhabited by lower races, – a racial aristocracy considered in their relation to the subject peoples, a democracy in their relation to each other.'

This definition is Rhodes doctrine pure and simple, and Buchan's as well. According to these two men, 'racial aristocracy', 'lower races' and 'empire' are the three great elements that in the right mix form world order.

I personally have read Buchan's fiction since I was a schoolboy. I swallowed him then uncritically as I swallowed Rider Haggard, whom I liked even more in those juvenile days. In my adulthood I came not merely to dislike, but positively to hate Buchan's and Haggard's *ex cathedra* statements and prejudices about race, even though they bestowed a spurious 'racial aristocracy' on me.

King Solomon's (Not Africa's) Mines

Mention of H. Rider Haggard carries one back to Victorian fiction, a genre that was free to exalt Englishness in frankly racist terms – a freedom now inhibited. Haggard, like Buchan, was an old Africa hand: a colonial administrator. *King Solomon's Mines* (1885) is an early tribute to Cecil Rhodes and his work, begun ten years earlier, to mine the diamond riches of Africa. Getting at the precious stones involved technical problems that Rhodes solved, with expert assistance, allowing him to set up De Beers consolidated mines in 1888 with funding from the Rothschild bank. In addition to technology, the mining involved cheap indigenous labour.

The plot of *King Solomon's Mines* is rattlingly simple. Allan Quatermain of Natal, a big-game hunter who knows the African interior like the back of his (bronzed) hand, is recruited to make up a party with Sir Henry Curtis and Captain John Good, in order to search for Curtis's younger brother, who is lost in the heart of the 'dark continent'. There's also a map, promising untold riches – diamonds, from King Solomon's fabled mines.

Accompanied by the necessary band of native bearers, the white men duly find and follow King Solomon's road, dodging tribal spears and surviving witchcraft (notably that practised by the sinister Gagool). They return to the motherland, enriched by pouches full of diamonds. Blood diamonds, we would call them, given the number of Africans slain in the novel.

The connection with Rhodes, for anyone who knows the magnate's career, is transparent, along with the novel's blithe assumption that Africa's mineral wealth does not belong to Africa but to the most ruthless European entrepreneurs. Recall Joseph Conrad's Kurtz, in *Heart of Darkness* (1899): 'all Europe contributed to the making of Kurtz'. And, should Africa resist, call in Edgar Wallace's *Sanders of the River*, who kept Africa in line with his Maxim gun and no-nonsense Hausa mercenaries whose humanity extends only to members of their own tribe.

In *King Solomon's Mines*, modern readers will also be struck by the casually wanton exploitation, not merely of Africa's mineral wealth, but of its natural riches. I remember in my unregenerate childhood reading days the primal thrill of Chapter Four, 'An Elephant Hunt', with its casual gunnery and white supremacy. The Englishmen slaughter virtually a whole herd, just for the pleasure of it, and 'after we were rested a little, and the Kafirs had cut out the hearts of two of the dead elephants for supper, we started homewards, very well pleased with our day's work.' Eight elephants they judge to be 'a pretty good bag'.

The African bush elephant now teeters on the brink of extinction. I have, as an adult, written a book-length lament for this finest and largest of land beasts and what our degraded species does to it.[81] It's a kind of apology for having once enjoyed Haggard's novel.

Lady Chatterley's Lover: 'Old England' is Gone Forever

D. H. LAWRENCE's last novel was a long time reaching the light of English publication. 'Lady Chat' (as it was chummily called in the swinging sixties) was written in the late 1920s, in Italy, as Lawrence was dying – and impotent, a central theme in the novel. It was published in Paris, and worked in subsequent years underground like a mole on English culture. Fiction written by dying authors, last will and testament fiction, has a peculiar force; see *Nineteen Eighty-four* or Virginia Woolf's *Between the Acts* (see 'Virginia Woolf's Farewell to England (and the World)' below). There's a 'This is all I have to say, goodbye world' about *Lady Chatterley's Lover*.

It is a pity that Lawrence's status in common parlance depends on a novel spattered with 'four-letter words' and what the Old Bailey prosecutors of the novel, in November 1960, called 'sexual bouts' – hanky-panky. The novel circulated in Paris (principally among English tourists) as a 'dirty book'. It was the French Olympia Press edition that I read, as a teenager, on my first trip to Paris. Other DBs (as their mischievous publisher, Maurice Girodias, called them), such as *Thongs* by Carmencita de las Lunas (actually Alexander Trocchi, a talented writer picking up a smudgy franc or two with a sado-masochistic fantasy), inspired a more kinetic response, I recall. It was interesting that in those days unillustrated books could do that.

Reading it today, one can see 'Lady Chat' as a profound novel about what Lawrence, in one of his short stories, called 'England, My England' (see below, *'England, England'*). The action centres on the woes of a British aristocrat, Sir Clifford Chatterley, whose family – in its later generations – has enriched itself from coal and, thereby, the enslavement of the working classes who mine the stuff (from which background, of course, Lawrence himself sprang) and do not get rich. British aristocrats, unlike their French and Russian counterparts, had no objection to a coal mine on their front lawn, so long as it meant cash. It is one reason the British top class has survived. Lawrence agreed with Carlyle that the contemporary generations of British aristocracy were a decadent top tier who had forgotten their national duty.

Sir Clifford Chatterley has been paralysed in action in the Great War. His brother Herbert, the heir to the Chatterley estate, is killed. Clifford, or what is left of him, returns to manage the family estates and the mines, paraplegic and in a wheelchair. The wheelchair, powered by steam, symbolizes Clifford's allegiance to the soullessly mechanical England in which he lives and by which he profits. He owns coal mines. He and his class have lost their power physically, but they can exercise it financially. Look at the *Sunday Times* 'rich list' – aristocrats with vast estates and land rents dominate.[82]

Clifford is not a villain, merely an example of what crippled England itself now is. The 'heroes' and 'great men' who made the country are no more. Constance, the wife Clifford chose before going off to battle, finds herself after the war in a blank marriage. Clifford is, effectively, a eunuch with a title. But there must, if his England is to survive, be an heir to whom to pass that title and his lands.

Clifford instructs his wife to choose a mate. A surrogate son, whose true paternity no one (perhaps not even he or she) knows, will ensure the Chatterley line. Constance, that is to say, must be inconstant, for the good of England. There is another pun in Lady Chat's nickname, 'Connie' – the C-word. She is a brood mare. Princess Diana, one speculates, may have felt something similar when she realized the nature of her marriage. Produce an heir apparent; after that, job done.

Instead of choosing someone of Clifford's own class for her sanctioned adulteries, Connie homes in on the estate game-keeper, Mellors. Why? Because Mellors truly represents the 'old England' she intuitively loves, an England that can be worshipped for its 'nature', not its machinery. He embodies that old, or 'merrie', England celebrated by poets going back to the country's origins. Call it the 'green and pleasant land':

Connie was accustomed to Kensington or the Scotch hills or the Sussex downs: that was her England. With the stoicism of the young she took in the utter, soulless ugliness of the coal-and-iron Midlands at a glance, and left it at what it was: unbelievable and not to be thought about. From the rather dismal rooms at Wragby she heard the rattle-rattle of the screens at the pit, the puff of the winding-engine, the clink-clink of shunting trucks, and the hoarse little whistle of the colliery loco-motives. Tevershall pit-bank was burning, had been burning for years, and it would cost thousands to put it out. So it had to burn. And when the wind was that way, which was often, the house was full of the stench of this sulphurous combustion of the earth's excrement. But even on windless days the air always smelt of something under-earth: sulphur, iron, coal, or acid. And even on the Christmas roses the smuts settled persistently, incredible, like black manna from the skies of doom.

Well, there it was: fated like the rest of things! It was rather awful, but why kick? You couldn't kick it away.

Connie bleakly accepts the awfulness of industrial England. She cannot change it; it is unkickable. As the narrative twists and complicates she realizes – as did Lawrence, the 'passionate pilgrim' – that there is only one solution: to escape to where the awfulness hadn't (yet) happened; Italy, or primitive South America. That is the only way one can 'come through'.[83]

Connie's realization builds to Lawrence's final testament about England, and the need either to cut and run or to find a way, if only symbolic, to return to 'Old England'. A useful exercise for those concerned with England's present situation is to call up the online version and search the 42 uses in the novel of 'England'.

In her transcendent moment of enlightenment, Connie casts an eye over the industrialized, mechanized 'wasteland' in which she is living (Lawrence had read T. S. Eliot's poem) and resolves to live instead in natural England with her gamekeeper lover. Her rejection of 'ladyship' and discovery of what it is to be a woman are crystallized as she looks out of the window of a limousine (limousines will, for her, soon be a thing of the past). What Lawrence gives us, through Connie's perceptions, is one of the finest scenes about fallen England to be found in English fiction:

> The car ploughed uphill through the long squalid straggle of Tevershall, the blackened brick dwellings, the black slate roofs glistening their sharp edges, the mud black with coal-dust, the pavements wet and black. It was as if dismalness had soaked through and through everything. The utter negation of natural beauty, the utter negation of the gladness of life, the utter absence of the instinct for shapely beauty which every bird and beast has, the utter death of the human intuitive faculty was appalling. The stacks of soap in the grocers' shops, the rhubarb and lemons in the greengrocers! the awful hats in the milliners! all went by ugly, ugly, ugly, followed by the plaster-and-gilt horror of the cinema with its wet picture announcements, 'A Woman's Love!', and

the new big Primitive chapel, primitive enough in its stark brick and big panes of greenish and raspberry glass in the windows. The Wesleyan chapel, higher up, was of blackened brick and stood behind iron railings and blackened shrubs. The Congregational chapel, which thought itself superior, was built of rusticated sandstone and had a steeple, but not a very high one. Just beyond were the new school buildings, expensive pink brick, and gravelled playground inside iron railings, all very imposing, and fixing the suggestion of a chapel and a prison. Standard Five girls were having a singing lesson, just finishing the la-me-doh-la exercises and beginning a 'sweet children's song'. Anything more unlike song, spontaneous song, would be impossible to imagine: a strange bawling yell that followed the outlines of a tune. It was not like savages: savages have subtle rhythms. It was not like animals: animals *mean* something when they yell. It was like nothing on earth, and it was called singing. Connie sat and listened with her heart in her boots, as Field was filling petrol. What could possibly become of such a people, a people in whom the living intuitive faculty was dead as nails, and only queer mechanical yells and uncanny will-power remained?

A coal-cart was coming downhill, clanking in the rain. Field started upwards, past the big but weary-looking drapers and clothing shops, the post-office, into the little market-place of forlorn space, where Sam Black was peering out of the door of the Sun, that called itself an inn, not a pub, and where the commercial travellers stayed, and was bowing to Lady Chatterley's car.

The church was away to the left among black trees. The car slid on downhill, past the Miners' Arms. It had already passed the Wellington, the Nelson, the Three Tuns, and the Sun, now it passed the Miners' Arms, then the Mechanics' Hall, then the new and almost gaudy Miners' Welfare and so, past a few new 'villas', out into the blackened road between dark hedges and dark green fields, towards Stacks Gate.

Tevershall! That was Tevershall! Merrie England! Shakespeare's England! No, but the England of today, as Connie had realized since she had come to live in it. It was producing a new race of mankind, over-conscious in the money and social and political side, on the spontaneous, intuitive side dead, but dead. Half-corpses, all of them: but with a terrible insistent consciousness in the other half. There was something uncanny and underground about it all. It was an under-world. And quite incalculable. How shall we understand the reactions in half-corpses? . . . And this was England, the vast bulk of England: as Connie knew, since she had motored from the centre of it.

Those thinking about Brexit should read with care this off-cut from a universally misread novel.

Obviously Connie yearns, inwardly, to return to 'Old England' – what balladry calls 'Merrie England' – but it is not there any more. Can it be restored? This touches on the deepest, and in its incoherent way the noblest of UKIP urges: the desire to make England again what it was. Can it be done? No. Is it worth trying? Yes.

The Amis Objection

T ellingly, Lawrence could not resolve the problems his
narrative raises. It will forever remain open-ended, an
unfinished story, with Mellors and Connie in a state of anxious
separation. *Lady Chatterley's Lover* is what the Victorians called
a 'Condition of England' novel.[84] But one of the reflections
arising from one's reading of it is whether 'Merrie England', a
utopia in the pre-industrial, pre-urban past, so clearly valued
by Lawrence, is just a myth, like the pot of gold at the end of
the rainbow. History suggests that 'merriment' probably never
existed other than in the imagination of posterity.

Such was the brutally satirical contradiction of Lawrence
that Kingsley Amis launched in *Lucky Jim* (1954). The novel's
'lucky' hero (at the end of it all) is a history lecturer, James
Dixon, at a third-rate 'provincial' (aka 'redbrick') university
(so-called). The place is never mentioned by name but it is iden-
tifiably Leicester, where Kingsley's best friend, Philip Larkin,
was marooned as an assistant librarian – a low form of life in
the university world of the 1950s. Amis, who like Larkin was
Oxford through and through (certified 'first class'), was similarly marooned in the second-rate mire (as Oxonians routinely
thought) of Swansea University. *Lucky Jim* came to him, he said,
on an inspirational visit to Leicester's seedy Senior Common
Room, inhabited as it was by seedy seniors.

In 1957, soon after *Lucky Jim* was published, Leicester got its
Charter and detached itself from London University to become
a university (not a mere 'university college') in its own right.
Britain had meanwhile lost the cod war against tiny Iceland and,
after the Suez debacle, lost any claim to be a serious world power.

Leicester is my alma mater; having received three degrees
from it, I revere the place. That is not relevant here. But I do

resent Amis's sneers. In his novel, Jim, who loathes his place of work (he doesn't in fact do much work as such), is charged by his obnoxious head of department to give a public lecture on 'Merrie England'.

Jim gets sloshed before the event and, swaying on the podium, begins reading his own lecture in the style of an ss book-burner reading the pacifist pamphlet of a Jewish communist. The episode is worthy of Jerome K. Jerome's *Three Men in a Boat*.

Finally Jim deserts his script, and reverts to his normal voice, to 'speak his mind' about bloody awful Merrie England. The passage is one of the most deliciously funny in English fiction. 'What, finally, is the practical application of all this?' Dixon asks 'in his normal voice':

> He felt he was in the grip of some vertigo, hearing himself talking without willing any words. 'Listen and I'll tell you. The point about Merrie England is that it was about the most un-Merrie period in our history. It's only the home-made pottery crowd, the organic husbandry crowd, the Esperanto . . .' He paused and swayed; the heat, the drink, the nervousness, the guilt at last joined forces in him.

Jim collapses, dead drunk, but he has made his statement. Old England was filthy, diseased and ignorant. Thank God it's past.

One wishes that Amis had lived long enough to get his teeth into Nigel Farage. But the question Lawrence vs Amis poses for those whose minds are currently engaged with Brexit is clear. Amis himself, in a tart letter to the *Telegraph* (his favourite paper, unsurprisingly) in the late 1970s, noted that the EU had produced no worthwhile literature yet, and that it would probably be some centuries before it did. If, that is, the ramshackle thing lasted that long.

Is Merrie England, the 'green and pleasant land', a delusion? Folk legend? Or is it something worth fighting for? Answers, please, in the voting booth.

Philip Larkin: The Greatest English Poet of Our Time

It seems like Larkin had long been preparing his English readership for Brexit.
AMIT CHAUDHURI[85]

How, then, would the poet's vote have gone had he lived to cast it? Leave, of course, along with the overwhelming majority in Hull, the city in which Larkin chose to pass his professional life (or let his life pass him) because, as he said, 'it's so far away from everywhere else.' By which he meant it was harder for foreigners to reach.

There's an iconic photograph of Philip Larkin sitting on a signpost that says, *tout court*, 'England'.[86] Voting with the buttocks, one might say. The photo was taken with Larkin's twin-lens Rolleiflex, one of the few things he loved that came from abroad. It was snapped by Monica Jones, whom he also loved (on and off; he was on and off a number of women), and it might well have been taken on the road from Melrose to Hexham, where she had a cottage in which the couple would occasionally stay. Hadrian's Wall is nearby. One can read something into that. It was not always as easy to cross the border as it is now; indeed perhaps, with Scottish independence always looming, it may never be as easy again as it is now.

Jones put a lot of lead in Larkin's pencil. In a historical period when travel was becoming ever freer, easier and cheaper, she proclaimed a visceral disdain for foreign places that Larkin took over. 'Would you like to visit, say, China?' a *Paris Review* interviewer inquired. 'I wouldn't mind seeing China', Larkin replied, 'if I could come back the same day. I hate being abroad.'

A big event of the year for the couple (particularly Jones) was the annual summer trip to Lord's cricket ground to see the MCC, not England, play whom ever was touring that year. The history of the place meant as much as leather and willow. Larkin was, I think, a member. I remember Monica saying how she loved the seal-like grace of Colin Cowdrey in the slips. Passionate as I was in my young days, I never liked Cowdrey myself for dodging his National Service with the excuse that he – one of the foremost athletes in the country – had fallen arches. But he had a gracious style with the bat and with his darting hands in the slips.

The West Indian and subcontinental cricketers were, one suspects, the only visitors of colour Larkin and Monica liked coming to Britain.[87] The others, as one of his much-quoted and most obnoxious private verses shows, he felt should be kicked out.

I recall Monica saying how much they had enjoyed a summer holiday on Sark, which, in my mind (I've never been there), has the same relation to metropolitan London that Devil's Island has to Paris. But for them it was an England stripped down to the elemental rock. What do they know of England who only England know? asks Kipling. Quite enough for Philip Larkin, thank you very much. And mind your own business.

There is, of course, infinitely more to the poet Larkin than the blimpishness of remarks such as only day trips to China being just about bearable. It's the comic-reverse side of an undying love for England. In a more serious mood in his prose volume *Required Writing*, Larkin put it more thoughtfully: 'Poetry and Sovereignty are very primitive things. I like to think of their being united in this way in England.' Sovereignty is the resonant word here. What Larkin is saying, as I understand it, is that nationhood and poetry are interfused. To write a good poem, on whatever subject, is to say something about England.

The word 'sovereignty' was much bandied about in the run-up to the June 2016 vote. It was not just fealty to Her Majesty the Sovereign (Larkin turned down her request to be her laureate). It meant something along the lines of 'England means England.'

Gloom is Larkin's literary climate. His poetry pictures an 'England Lost' whose decayed and ever-decaying state is, nonetheless, preferable to anywhere else available on the planet. Certainly China. Where, then, was this lost England to be found? In the past, self-evidently. One can put a date to its losing, and this his year-dated poem does precisely. It is entitled 'MCMXIV', a numeral one would normally see on a gravestone. In the elegy for an 'innocent' England gone forever, written in 1960, Larkin describes the baking summer (meteorologically correct) of 1914, the queues waiting patiently outside the Oval cricket ground, the 'moustached archaic faces', the pubs open all day, children named, patriotically, after kings and queens. The images pile up, artistically, to an Edenic England that can only exist, not in memory or historical record, but in romance. But romance – even in the voting booth – is potent.

Like William Golding, Larkin believed that world war, as perfected in the twentieth century, injected poison into a nation's being for ever and a day. For Golding, the fatal dose was the Second World War, in which he served (Larkin was too frail). For Larkin, it was the 'the war they call great', which marked the great historical threshold between Olde England and Fallen England. He was born in 1922, and in his early childhood could still catch whiffs of that great 1914–18 bloodletting. There would be, he prophesied, a third war – the Russian tank guns were all pointed westward. Then it would all be over. No

Channel guns would save Hardy's country; there would be no more England.

One of the things that will strike a Brexiteer coming to a poem such as 'MCMXIV' is how comprehensible its English is. Along with Ted Hughes and Thom Gunn, Larkin is placed by literary historians as one of the leading members of a 1960s group of poets called 'The Movement', who advocated a return to traditionally English verse.

The truth is that Larkin had no intention of moving an inch from the English tradition embodied by Thomas Hardy (he kept Hardy's *Collected Poetry* on his bedside table) and, at a lower level of achievement, John Betjeman. He disliked the modernism that (following Eliot) had transformed English poetry, believing that it was a stylistic immigrant, an invasion from Europe and America.

To return to Chaudhuri's quotation with which we began. He continues:

> Well before the European Economic Community came into existence in 1957, Larkin was espousing the virtues of 'leaving' and of separateness. His extraordinary and strikingly small body of verse must now be seen as a significant, undeniable and vivid component in the cultural history of the leave camp.

One could, I think, rate Larkin's body of verse higher than a mere 'component'. It is the spirit of Leave expressed, and monumentalized, in exquisite verse.

Postscript: Hockney

After the referendum David Hockney (a staunch and loudly outspoken Leave proponent) pondered how 'British cultural giants' of the past would have voted. Hockney, one recalls, designed a special masthead for the *Sun* newspaper, UKIP's ear-shattering megaphone. He concluded that the most admirable of the BCGs would, as sure as eggs is eggs, have voted his way, and he expanded to give chapter and verse.

In February 2017 Hockney's popular retrospective opened at Tate Britain in London. An undeniable cultural giant himself, he observed, somewhat enigmatically, 'The power has spread to the people because that's what the iPhone has done.'[88] But the point was that the people knew what they wanted and had expressed their will in June 2016.

Alan Bennett, a figure of equal cultural gigantism but of a radically opposite opinion to Hockney's, wrote, the day of the epochal vote, in his diary: 'I imagine this must have been what Munich was like in 1938 – half the nation rejoicing at a supposed deliverance, the other half stunned by the country's self-serving cowardice.'[89] And what dark Hitler was about to rise from the swamp?

It was extraordinary. Leave/Remain had sliced the country's intelligentsia (BCGs) in half like an over-ripe apple. Is this how once-great countries end, or is it the prelude to phoenix-like regeneration?

Why the Brexiteer Loves Sherlock

Why does the man in the deerstalker, with beaky nose and magnifying glass, still enchant us, and most of all, one suspects, the detective-story-loving Brexiteer? On the face of it, Arthur Conan Doyle's stories and novels require a quite remarkable tolerance for nonsensicality (so, on occasion, does Brexit, partisans might claim). As the websites that place importance on such Doylean things (such as www.

bestofsherlock.com) tell us, the most popular of Doyle's short stories is 'The Speckled Band', which features a serpent that climbs up and down bell ropes to kill young ladies on command. Pull the other one. 'The Adventure of the Blue Carbuncle' (No. 5 on the popularity poll) is not, you may be surprised to know, about Dr Doyle doing a Victorian version of the TV show *Embarrassing Bodies*. Murder by jellyfish? Holmes cracks that one in 'The Adventure of the Lion's Mane'.

Doyle was, famously, torn to shreds in one of the funniest hatchet jobs in literary history, Edmund Wilson's essay 'Mr Holmes, They Were the Footprints of an Enormous Hound!' A baronet is frightened to death by a dog, bought in the Fulham Road, whose eyes some sadist (unidentified) has daubed with phosphorus, making them glow demonically. Why not just toss Sir Henry Baskerville into Grimpen Mire? The mud tells no tales.

It is the resident couple in 221B Baker Street (they're gay, it's whispered knowingly nowadays; did Doyle know?) who have the unique honour of London's most venerable Underground station being decorated in their memory with Holmesiana. I seem to recall the homicidal jellyfish is there on one of the ceramic panels.

In literary historical terms, the ancestral figure is Edgar Allan Poe, in whose work originated the solving of crimes based on ratiocination and, in Auguste Dupin, the unofficial detective smart enough to ratiocinate. Forget flatfoots like Inspector Lestrade. He would never have worked out that, in Poe's most famous story, it was a homicidal orangutan that stuffed the corpses up the chimney.

The link between Victorian doctors' increasing sophistication in 'reading' symptoms in the sick and Victorian detectives' increasing skill in interpreting 'clues' is a literary critical commonplace. As most of us know, Sherlock Holmes owes his major debt in this regard less to Poe than to the physician who taught the future Dr Arthur Conan Doyle at Edinburgh University. Joseph Bell was a symptomatologist of genius. He would cast an eye on a new patient in his surgery and, without physical examination, tell them they had manifestly come to him on a number 79 bus but had not bought their ticket, that they had not changed their underpants in three days, and that they were probably worried about a small growth as yet uncovered on their knee. Bell's 'inductive' method became famous, not least from Doyle's descriptions of it.

Bell did not just look at his patients. For the diagnosis of diphtheria he developed a pipette – long tube – to suck telltale pus from the sufferer's throat. On one unlucky occasion he sucked too hard; he infected himself, nearly died and had a voice that sounded funny for the rest of his life. We should all have such conscientious healers.

We come at last to the answer to the question I ask above. The main reason the Brexiteer loves Sherlock Holmes is his amateurism. He does detection the same way he does the violin, amateurishly. We never know where his income comes from, but Sherlock does not work. He studied at university but never bothered with degrees. He's amateurism incarnate.

I'm old enough to remember the annual Gentlemen (amateurs) versus Players (professionals) games of cricket. Only 'gentlemen' could captain the national team in those days. It was an English institution (the Scots, Welsh and Northern Irish have no national teams) until the English nation got fed up with being trounced by Aussies.

But amateurism was what it meant truly to 'represent' England. As, God bless him, does Holmes – at least for nostalgists. And there are no greater adherents to nostalgia – Olde England – than the Brexiteers.

Mad Dogs and Englishmen (and Jeeves)

W ith the foregoing Sherlockian theme in mind, take a moment to ponder other national stereotypes relevant to *Homo brexitus*. The lyrics fall flat when transcribed on the page, but cock an ear, via YouTube, to Noël Coward's song about what makes the English absurd to foreign eyes – yet mysteriously all-conquering: 'Mad Dogs and Englishmen'.[90]

The lyrics are a half-rhymed cascade of comic racialism (to be honest, some of it has become distinctly un-comic since 1931). The song opens, in Coward's chirping voice, with a cartoon pic of tropical johnnies tearing off their clothing when the sun blazes. But the English, and mad dogs, go out in the noonday sun. Other nations (by which Coward means races) are, the ditty tells us, welcome to giggle as the English heel comes down on their neck. But, laugh as you will, at its imperial height (around the end of Victoria's reign) that wet handkerchief, as Ernest Hemingway called England, owned two-thirds of the earth.[91]

When Farage said to the European Parliament, after the referendum: 'you're not laughing now,' he forbore to ape Coward by ejaculating 'Ha ha ha ha hoo hoo hoo hoo hee hee hee hee', although something like it was visible on his televised face. (Which, incidentally, has always reminded me of Buster Keaton, who can still raise a laugh.)

The other stereotype, summoned in his case by the silver bell, is – of course – Jeeves. Other nations have their Sancho Panzas (peasantly shrewd), their Figaros (here, there, everywhere), their Sam Spade 'sidekicks', their valets (to whom no man is hero), their factota, their 'celebrity' PAS, their Passepartouts, their Moscas. The 'witty servant' (smarter than his master) can be traced back to the Latin dramatist Terence, but only one nation has the omnicompetent butler, the gentleman's gentleman.

Codes of service define nations, and the butler embodies a core element of England, although very few English households can afford one.

Jeeves, the most famous butler in literature, was conceived by P. G. 'Plum' Wodehouse in the early post-war period, when Englishness, after the awfulness of the trenches (and feared Revolution, Russian-style), needed a restorative boost of 100 per cent Albion. That authorial nickname 'Plum' tells us much of what we need to know about the writer.[92] So does the fact that Wodehouse did not divulge Jeeves's Christian name until 56 years after he was first introduced ('Reginald', we learned).[93]

Servants, of which butlers are the highest class, have one-word labels, and no genealogy. A stork drops them off anywhere it spies a town mansion, palace or rolling country estate. Jeeves has become the synonym for 'butler' (women have to make do with 'girl Friday'). But the term needs some modification. He does indeed 'buttle' when needs must, but Jeeves is a more intimate attender to his employer Bertie (Bertram) Wooster's person. He is a *valet de chambre* – a man's man.

Bertie Wooster, by contrast, has a Christian name, a nickname and a formidable pedigree. There are thousands of words on the fictional Wooster family on Wikipedia. The only point to recall, when reading, is that he was orphaned early and left very rich, by which one means idle rich. After an unoppressive education at Eton and Oxford (Bullingdon membership we can safely suppose), Bertie graduates to the aptly named Drones Club in Mayfair to work seriously on his daily idleness.

Most people – particularly Hollywood people – think butlers are very Olde Englishe. The term certainly is, but the modern image of a flunkey bringing an ironed copy of *The Times* on a silver tray with a 'Will there be anything else, sir?' in a strangulated accent as abnormal as Darth Vader's isn't, alas, originally and entirely English.

The word 'butler' originates in the Old French *bouteleur* (cup-bearer), from *bouteille* (bottle). These were upper servants trusted not to poison the master – something of a hazard in Old France, apparently. William the Conqueror probably brought the primal butler to England via Hastings, along with his crew of lesser bottle-washers, and, of course, a barber (from the French for 'beard').

The image of 'ye olde Englishe butler' was popularized by J. M. Barrie's play *The Admirable Crichton* (1902). It continues to be popularized, to the present day, in high literature such as Kazuo Ishiguro's *The Remains of the Day* (see 'The End of Jeeves' below) and in low fiction such as *Batman*, where (Alfred) Pennyworth (played most recently, radically against his born accent, by Michael Caine) 'does' for his billionaire master, Bruce Wayne. Somewhere in between Ishiguro's Mr Stevens and Pennyworth is Mr Carson of *Downton Abbey*.

I always think the Conservative MP Jacob Rees-Mogg – pro-Brexit to his Savile Row fly buttons – must have a butler, having outgrown the nanny who loyally accompanied him, as the press reported with relish, on his early campaigning days. Bally stupid fellow. And by Jiminy, as I write he's being propelled by 'Moggmentum' towards Downing Street.

The first of many collections of Jeeves and Wooster stories came out in 1925. At the start of the opening story, 'Jeeves Takes Charge', Bertram ('Bertie') has just fired his previous valet for 'sneaking my silk socks, a thing no bloke of spirit could stick at any price'. He has asked the agency for a replacement less prone to such insufferable larcenies.

Bertie wakes with a 'morning head' to find a 'kind of darkish sort of respectful Johnnie' at the door. He has a 'grave, sympathetic face' and an ability to glide, soundlessly, not 'clump'. Bertie's head is too sore to accept any clumping. Jeeves's first act is to mix an infallible hangover cure of raw egg, Worcester sauce and pepper. (The recipe went on to become legendary as the Prairie Oyster – Wodehouse could have made another pretty penny marketing that remedy with his face on it, like Paul Newman's salad dressing.) For a moment Bertie 'felt as if somebody had touched off a bomb inside the old bean', and then 'everything seemed suddenly to get all right'. Jeeves, destroyer of hangovers, is hired on the spot.

He goes on to be similarly invaluable at a country-house weekend, where the inept Bertie has been charged by his imperious fiancée to do a Raffles on the manuscript of a dangerously frank memoir that a senior member of the household intends to publish. Jeeves takes charge and, in the process, breaks his master's engagement to the young lady of the house ('You would not have been happy, sir!') while discreetly disposing of an 'unsuitable' checked suit to the under-gardener. The pattern is set. Bertie, 'bally idiot' that he is, gets into some 'bloomin' scrape' and the omnicompetent Jeeves comes to the rescue and, brooking no contradiction, decrees what his master simply must wear. Who is the man and who the master? The question often perplexes Bertie.

It would be a most regrettable error to see what Jeeves represents as merely a classic caricature of English quaintness. Brexit has, within it, a reverence for Jeevesiana. There is no way of knowing, but one's instincts suggest that the bulk of the huge viewing audience for *Downton Abbey* is, in part, tribute to what Carson represents, 'Englishness'. An England that is hanging together, organically, all its parts fitting one another. Hierarchically. Downton is based on Highclere Castle in Hampshire, a county that voted, solid as a rock, to Leave (see 'Jane Austen's "England"', above).

The End of Jeeves

It took a gifted novelist, born in Nagasaki but a British citizen since 1983, to point out the fact of the end of Jeeves in his elegiacally titled Booker Prize-winning novel *The Remains of the Day* (1989). What Jeeves embodied is no more; all we have left to warm our English selves with are embers and the dying warmth of a setting sun. Remains. No more mad dogs and Englishmen, or empires over which the sun never sets, no more global maps red with conquest. The British Empire, once the largest the world has ever known, has not declined and fallen – like Gibbon's Rome – but faded into grey nonentity, becoming a shell of its old self.

The hero of Ishiguro's novel is a butler whose world, call it England, is decaying around him. It is 1956, which means the Suez Crisis, the moment when the British really lost their empire. After 1956, said Malcolm Bradbury, 'barbarism' took over (incarnated as the 'history man' Howard Kirk). The Brexiteer should think deeply about Jeeves and Stevens, about what makes them, like their literary patriarch Crichton, 'admirable', and about what their passing poignantly represents. Can it be, somehow, in some form, recovered? By a cross in the right box?

Ishiguro's narrative takes the form of inner reminiscence by an ancient butler, a trusty but somewhat tongue-tied retainer at Darlington Hall. He too is decaying. Stevens is given a holiday and permission to use the Hall's venerable Ford by Darlington's new American owner, Mr Farraday. Car keys in hand, Stevens resolves to make an 'expedition' to the West Country, where he will meet a former employee of the Hall, Miss Kenton, a housekeeper who left twenty years earlier. There was once the possibility that the two of them might have been in love, but they fell out over an obscure below-stairs dispute. Their respective professional susceptibilities were mortally affronted, and they have not communicated since she left in a huff.

Stevens has recently begun to detect in himself 'small errors' in the performance of his duties. His edge has gone. He hopes that Miss Kenton (now Mrs Benn) can be persuaded to return to the Hall. With her help, he may be able to hold things together for a few more years. A letter from her, hinting at marital unhappiness, gives him grounds for hope that reconciliation and below-stairs alliance, as before, are possible.[94]

The novel takes the form of a six-day *journal de voyage* through mid-1950s England. The meeting with the former Miss Kenton in Weymouth is a disappointment. Her marriage is indeed unhappy; she has frequently walked out on her husband. But she has no intention of walking back to the Hall: 'My rightful place is with my husband. After all, there's no turning back the clock now. One can't be for ever dwelling on what might have been. One should realise one has as good as most, perhaps better, and be grateful.' Sound advice. 'At that moment, my heart was breaking,' Stevens tells us. But he gives no sign of it. Butlers do not show their feelings; imperturbability is the badge of all their tribe. His 'rightful place', he resolves, is at the Hall, where he will serve his time as best he can, 'small errors' and all. He takes strength from a chance encounter with a stranger whom he meets, walking along the seafront at evening. Stevens blurts out his misery: 'I gave my best to Lord Darlington. I gave him the very best I had to give, and now – well – I find I do not have a great deal more left to give.' His new-found friend advises: 'You've got to enjoy yourself. The evening's the best part of the day. You've done your day's work. Now you can put your feet up and enjoy it.' Duly bucked up, Stevens resolves to return to Mr Farraday's service in what he thinks of as a 'bantering' spirit. It is gallant but, as we apprehend, doomed. Stevens can no more banter than he can fly in the air.

Over the course of the six days' confessions, we gradually put together a portrait of the dignified, decaying, noble 'upper servant'– his little snobberies, intense professional pride, essential goodness and ineradicable, but lovable, stupidity. It has, for example, entirely escaped his notice that his former master, Lord Darlington, was a Mosley-sympathizing fascist. Stevens, we deduce, is the best of 'his' England, an England that will, like him, inevitably be no more. He is ahistorical. 'There's no turning back the clock now,' as Miss Kenton that was says.

That painful sense of things lost, we apprehend, was one of the drivers of the astonishing national decision on 23 June 2016 to saw off the limb, growing for forty years, that joined us to Europe. But which side were we sitting on, trunk or branch? We shall know all too soon.

Invasion by Immigration – From Calais, Mars or Wherever

Immigration has always been UKIP's trump card. Foreigners are 'swamping' us, as the Iron Lady put it in 1978 (at a time when immigration was under 100,000), turning a country into a swamp. This is Thatcher's full text:

> Well now, look, let us try and start with a few figures as far as we know them ... there was a committee which looked at it and said that if we went on as we are then by the end of the century there would be four million people of the new Commonwealth or Pakistan here. Now, that is an awful lot and I think it means that people are really rather afraid that this country might be rather swamped by people with a different culture and, you know, the British character has done so much for

democracy, for law and done so much throughout the world that if there is any fear that it might be swamped people are going to react and be rather hostile to those coming in.

Don't call it immigration, call it invasion. The equation is common in Brexit-speak.

Churchill put it more bluntly, and in high Churchillian English:

Turning once again, and this time more generally, to the question of invasion, I would observe that there has never been a period in all these long centuries of which we boast when an absolute guarantee against invasion, still less against serious raids, could have been given to our people. In the days of Napoleon, of which I was speaking just now, the same wind which would have carried his transports across the Channel might have driven away the blockading fleet. There was always the chance, and it is that chance which has excited and befooled the imaginations of many Continental tyrants. Many are the tales that are told. We are assured that novel methods will be adopted, and when we see the originality of malice, the ingenuity of aggression, which our enemy displays, we may certainly prepare ourselves for every kind of novel stratagem and every kind of brutal and treacherous manœuvre. I think that no idea is so outlandish that it should not be considered and viewed with a searching, but at the same time, I hope, with a steady eye. We must never forget the solid assurances of sea power and those which belong to air power if it can be locally exercised.

It was reported in *The Telegraph* on 28 February 2014 that Nigel Farage had brought the immigration/invasion anxiety up to the twenty-first century by declaring that immigration had left Britain 'unrecognisable':

> The Ukip leader told how he went on a commuter train journey recently through south east London and did not hear anyone speaking English, leaving him feeling 'awkward' and 'uncomfortable'.
>
> He said: 'Do I think parts of Britain are a foreign land? I got the train the other night, it was rush hour, from Charing Cross.
>
> 'It was a stopper going out and we stopped at London Bridge, New Cross, Hither Green, it was not til we got past Grove Park that I could hear English being audibly spoken in the carriage.'[95]

A rich energy source for the chauvinism throbbing in the heart of the Kippers is this fantasy of invasion – or of immigration so massive that it amounts to much the same thing.

It was the literary critic (and former military intelligence man) I. F. Clarke who pointed out that invasion fantasy is also one of the three or four core elements of science fiction.[96] As Clarke surveyed British science fiction, the genre began in its modern form with *The Battle of Dorking* (1871) by Colonel G. T. Chesney.

Chesney's fictional booklet, chronicling a successful invasion of England by the Germans, was inspired by the Prussian invasion of France a few months earlier. Soon all Europe would be German. Horrible thought. *The Battle of Dorking* sold like wildfire at a shilling a copy, and inspired a national panic: would England be next to feel the jackboot on its neck? Gladstone himself was obliged to warn against 'alarmism' and reassure the nation that John Bull, while he was in charge, would never submit to the Prussian invader. Just let the Kaiser try it!

Chesney's invasion fantasy fired off a fruitful line of dystopia and science fiction. 'Novel methods' (as Churchill calls them) were ingeniously imagined. All of them had, as their essence, the fearful idea that Britain's green and pleasant land would be, to repeat Mrs Thatcher's term, 'swamped' by aliens.

Of the two enduring invasion fantasies, M. P. Shiel's *The Yellow Peril* (first serialized in 1898 as *The Yellow Danger*) is now little read, but the phrase has entered common parlance. The other is H. G. Wells's *The War of the Worlds* (1897), a work that has been adapted many times for radio (famously by Orson Welles), TV and cinema.[97]

The period in which Wells wrote his 'scientific romance' is important. Britain was panicked not by Chesney's Huns but by immigration. Vast tides of refugees had been loosed on British shores by anti-Semitic pogroms and persecution in Russia and Middle Europe, leading to the Aliens Act 1905 – a pulling-up-the-drawbridge measure.

Wells took the term 'alien' more literally than did legislators of the time. The opening of *The War of the Worlds* is magnificent:

No one would have believed in the last years of the nineteenth century that this world was being watched keenly and closely by intelligences greater than man's and yet as mortal as his own; that as men busied themselves about their various concerns they were scrutinised and studied, perhaps almost as narrowly as a man with a microscope might scrutinise the transient creatures that swarm and multiply in a drop of water. With infinite complacency men went to and fro over this globe about their little affairs, serene in their assurance of their empire over matter. It is possible that the infusoria under the microscope do the same. No one gave a thought to the older worlds of space as sources of human danger, or thought of them only to dismiss the idea of life upon them as impossible or improbable. It is curious to recall some of the mental habits of those departed days. At moſt terreſtrial men fancied there might be other men upon Mars, perhaps inferior to themselves and ready to welcome a missionary enterprise. Yet across the gulf of space, minds that are to our minds as ours are to those of the beaſts that perish, intellects vaſt and cool and unsympathetic, regarded this earth with envious eyes, and slowly and surely drew their plans againſt us. And early in the twentieth century came the great disillusionment.

The Martians, driven by the desertification of their planet (why on earth does NASA want to waste billions going there?) and assisted by their superior military technology, set out to colonize Earth.

One says 'Earth'. But for some inscrutable reason (they make no attempt to learn our languages – typical immigrants) the Martians, from 40 million miles away, seem particularly interested in Woking. Their first cylinders land on the common. As does Dorking (the assonance was not, one may assume, accidental), Woking represents durable England: 'Homeland', as the Americans now call it. Tom Cruise, biceps and eyeballs bulging, was having none of it in the most recent film version, in which the Martian invasion targets the Big Apple.

The nameless narrator of Wells's romance, a Chobham man, is writing a paper on morality, a subject rendered meaningless by the realpolitik of the Martians. After the inadequate resistance of human artillery and ironclads (new, steel-armoured Royal Navy battleships) in a dramatic Thames estuary scene, the enemy's amphibious fighting machines, heat rays and poison smoke win an easy victory. Humanity might as well resist the invader with peashooters.

In his desperate flight and his struggle to reach his wife at Leatherhead, the narrator has a series of adventures. The Martians, green slimeballs that they (literally) are, have an appetite for human blood. Finally, in the wasteland of London the invaders fall victim to what else? Bugs. Bacilli, that is. Wells uses a striking 'as ye reap so shall ye sow' analogy:

> And before we judge of them too harshly we must remember what ruthless and utter destruction our own species has wrought, not only upon animals, such as the vanished bison and the dodo, but upon its inferior races. The Tasmanians, in spite of their human likeness, were entirely swept out of existence in a war of extermination waged by European immigrants, in the space of fifty years. Are we such apostles of mercy as to complain if the Martians warred in the same spirit?

Woking is saved by its microbial ally. The town voted staunchly Remain in June 2016.

Dracula: Illegal Immigrant

At the time of writing, mid-2017, it is reckoned that there are 70,000 Romanian workers in London, many of them in the construction industry, helping to regenerate the city and support their families at home in the process. In my experience they are skilled workers and good Europeans – even though they may add to the train-carriage Babel that, as Nigel Farage complains, casts a pall over the English language to such distant outposts as Grove Park.

How many famous Romanians can you name? A famous (but not world-famous) footballer or two, perhaps. The disgusting tyrant Ceaușescu (a knight of the realm, no less, an honour awarded by a reluctant Queen Elizabeth when we were sucking up to the brute and his virago wife). And, of course, Bram Stoker's Count Dracula, boyar of Transylvania.

The Romanian count is the archetypal illegal immigrant. He chooses to smuggle himself into England by a Russian cargo vessel (which he wrecks en route) bound for Whitby. Why that remote town? The answer is obvious, and it's not to visit the ruined abbey or drink in the wonderful coastal landscape – or to work on building sites. Had Dracula come to one of Britain's main ports of entry – Dover or Southampton, for example – there would have been customs and immigration officials, curious to see his papers, asking awkward questions about why a count, no less, would need fifty large boxes, no less, of Romanian dirt in his luggage.

Like Wells's Martians, the Count is a bloodsucking illegal immigrant. Doubtless, since he is long-lived (eternal if he avoids stakes through his heart and beheading; not a great risk in London) he will survive to the present day to get free prescriptions (16 gallons of plasma, please, Mr Chemist) on the NHS. Oh, and his seven-hundred-year-old teeth fixed, free of charge.

Dracula chooses to stay temporarily, metamorphosed into a large black dog when convenient to rip out a throat or two, in the woods round Whitby, until his boxes of dirt are in place in fifty safe houses around the capital. His bedding seen to, the Count sets out on his mission: sucking good English blood while having his way with good English maidens. Stoker does not specify his sexual habits; innumerable B-movies do, in detail. As an immigrant, Dracula is the very stuff online *Daily Mail* stories are made of. Doubtless at some point in his centuries-long stay he'll arrange to scrounge English benefits, as well.

But, the question arises, pressingly, why on earth does Dracula come to England? Not for gold – he has plenty of that, and a castle (with three barely garbed sirens) to go with it. Are there not throats enough in his native Transylvania to satisfy an undead's toothy appetites?

His reason for immigrating is to be found, I would suggest, by looking at the large number of spikily contemporary references in Stoker's text to recent gadgetry, communications technology and scientific innovation – things in whose invention and use England then led the world. It is significant, for example, that Jonathan Harker records his journal in shorthand. Later, he refers in passing to his 'Kodak', with which he has photographed the English estate that Dracula intends to buy. Mina, we are told, is learning to 'stenograph', so that when she marries Jonathan she can be his 'typewriter girl'. There are numerous references to the New Woman vogue, something that peaked in 1894 (Mina, although an advanced member of her sex, draws the line at aligning herself with New Women, what with their outrageous 'open sexual unions' and, worse still, sapphic practices). Lucy Westenra's life is prolonged, but not saved, by a blood transfusion (this is one of many references to up-to-the-minute medical advances; Stoker also includes references to brain surgery, for example). Lucy's phonograph cylinders are used by Dr Seward to make memoranda. Van Helsing even develops an early version of radar, employing Mina's powers as a mesmeric medium to locate the fleeing monster.

For his part, Dracula hates modernity – or, at least, he is nervous of it. Something might be invented by these fiendishly smart Englanders to kill vampires. He cannot read shorthand, and throws Harker's encrypted writings on the fire in disgust;

he chooses to come to England by sail, not steamboat; he studiously avoids the railway for the transport of his earth-filled boxes, choosing instead gypsy carts. What this means is that in the struggle between Van Helsing and Dracula, we have a contest between the 'pagan world of old' and 'modernity'. A demon from the Dark Ages is pitted against men of the 1890s armed with Winchester rifles, telegrams, phonographs, modern medicine and science. Stoker's Transylvania is certainly Gothic and ahistorical, but his England is as up-to-date as that week's edition of *Tit-Bits* magazine.

Why then, to repeat the question, does Dracula want to come to England? It would seem he has something more than tourism in mind. When we first encounter him, through Harker, he is practising his English in order to render it flawless, and is studying

> books . . . of the moſt varied kind – hiſtory, geography, politics, political economy, botany, geology, law – all relating to England and English life and cuſtoms and manners. There were even such books of reference as the London Directory, the 'Red' and 'Blue' books, Whitaker's Almanac, the Army and Navy Liſts, and – it somehow gladdened my heart to see it – the Law Liſt.

One apprehends from this that Dracula does not want to visit England; he wants to invade it, conquer it, make it his own infernal kingdom. And in the process he wants to learn to use for his own purposes English scientific and technological know-how.

The talkative Van Helsing discerns this reason for Dracula's coming to England late in the narrative. 'Do you not see', he asks Harker, 'how, of late, this monster has been creeping into knowledge experimentally?' Dracula, in other words, is learning how to think scientifically. The perspicacious professor elaborates the point a little later:

> With the child-brain that was to him he have long since conceive the idea of coming to a great city. What does he do? He find out the place of all the world moſt of promise for him. Then he deliberately set himself down to prepare for the task. He find in patience juſt how is his ſtrength, and what are his powers. He ſtudy new tongues. He learn new social life; new environment of old ways, the politic, the law, the finance, the science, the habit of a new land and a new people who have come to be since he was. His glimpse that he have had, whet his appetite only and enkeen his desire. Nay, it help him to grow as to his brain; for it all prove to him how right he was at the firſt in his surmises. He have done this alone; all alone! from a ruin tomb in a forgotten land. What more may he not do when the greater world of thought is open to him?

Dracula, we apprehend, has chosen England because it is the most modern country in the world – the most modern, that is, in its social organization, its industry, its education, its science. Small as the island is, compared to the vastness of Transylvania it is a world leader. To put it in its most banal form, he has come to England to learn how to use the Kodak, how to write in short-hand and how to operate the recording phonograph, in order that he may make himself a thoroughly modern vampire for the imminent twentieth century.

God Loves England (Does He Not?)

E ngland (other national regions of the UK less so) indulged in an orgiastic national retrospect during the centenary of the beginning of the First World War – the War called Great – in 2014. It was poppy day and two-minute silences all year round. 'Experience Passchendaele' invited one to a Sensurround podcast on the anniversary of that bloodbath. On the whole, it was something one would rather not experience. The BBC marinated its service to the country with memorialism. There was, overhanging it all, a sense that the war, like other extremities, had brought out the essence of Britain, despite its being a conflict whose rightness on either side was as clear as mud.

Ironically, the supreme leaders of England and Germany were closely related as members of the Saxe-Coburg (German) royal clan. The English branch, sharing a name with a German cake (Battenberg), promptly renamed itself after something else: Windsor soup. Very English.

The intense focus on the First World War, and commemorations of it, had a complex connection with the concurrent rise of Brexit. No one noticed the connection in the anniversary year, but it was clear as day in 2015.

It is worthwhile, in this context, for the Brexiteer to ponder one of the country's most popular texts (one can't quite call it a novel – more a sermon in fiction) written in the year 1914, 'The Bowmen' by Arthur Machen. The story has a simple message, and one that still reverberates a hundred years later. That message, very simply, is that God loves the English more than He loves the Hun, or any other race, come to that. He always has. The Spanish come to our shores with the biggest war navy ever built and *Deus afflavit* – God blew them away with His great storm. What is King Hal's battle cry as he leads his men into victory against the French? 'God for Harry, England and St George!' Did those feet, asks Blake's 'Jerusalem' (meaning our Saviour's plates of meat), walk on England's green and pleasant land? Yes, yes, says legend. Jesus loves England, just as his Father did and does.

War was declared between Britain and Germany in August 1914, and a British Expeditionary Force was dispatched across the Channel. Jingoism on the home front reached hysteria level. The BEF was outnumbered and ordered to defend positions against the invading Germans, which they had no time to fortify. Theirs not to reason why. These seasoned regulars – who had shot everything from 'fuzzy wuzzies' to 'Johnny Boer' (conscription of the British young had not yet cranked up, and wouldn't until 1917) – were the backbone of the BEF. With wry and characteristically English humour, they christened themselves 'the Old Contemptibles', throwing Kaiser Bill's insult (that their resistance was 'contemptible') back in his face.

At Mons, on the Belgian border, the BEF held their ground, stalling the enemy, before effecting an orderly retreat. The War Office called it 'strategic withdrawal'. Military history, taking a larger view, calls it a defeat, but, like Dunkirk in the Second World War, it was celebrated on the home front as somehow glorious.

Machen, a writer with a strong line in *fin de siècle* supernatural fiction, had, along with the rest of the nation, been gripped by wartime newsreel (this was the first war to be cinematically covered) and newspaper coverage. He was inspired to write his short story for the London *Evening News* of 29 September 1914. The narrative features a 'Latin scholar' on the front line, facing the Teutonic foe, who invokes the spirit of Henry v:

> as the Latin scholar uttered his invocation he felt something between a shudder and an electric shock pass

through his body. The roar of the battle died down in his ears to a gentle murmur; instead of it, he says, he heard a great voice and a shout louder than a thunder-peal crying, 'Array, array, array!'

Enter Harry's archers in 1914. Their longbows help to repel the Hun horde, some of whom, to the mystification of the German invader's *Feldlazarett* (field hospital) corps, have arrow wounds when their corpses are examined. 'Mein Gott!' No, Fritz, our God.

Machen's text is laced with the 'buckets of eyeballs' propaganda about German beastliness that had been wholly confected by the British dark propaganda authorities to induce the necessary bloodlust among a population who, in summer 1914, could not quite work out why a world war was necessary. A particularly vivid scene involves German soldiers crucifying a baby on a church door: 'The baby was only three years old. He died calling piteously for "mummy" and "daddy".' Swine.

The newspaper did not clearly label 'The Bowmen' as a work of fiction. Publication yielded Machen only a few pounds, but, in the weeks after it appeared, he was asked many times (mainly by clergymen, injecting war spirit into their sermons) for the right to reprint or recite his 'story'. They assumed it was a newspaper (fact-based) story, not a fairy tale for adults, which is what Machen had knowingly produced.

'The Bowmen' merged with a confluent stream of war propaganda reporting that, during the Battle of Mons, British soldiers had merely seen not archers but 'angels' assisting their heroic efforts. Angels/Angeli: the homonym went back to Roman times. Angels love us too.

It has been plausibly suggested that this nonsense was subversively egged on by 'black arts' propagandists in the war ministry. In wartime, populations go collectively gaga, and their superiors encourage it. Robert Graves, the poet serving at the front, called it 'the inward scream, the duty to run mad'. In his memoir of the war, *Good-bye to All That* (1929), he records seeing no divine reinforcement or angels in British khaki. Just mess.

Machen reissued his story ten months later, plumped out to novel length with news reports, as *The Angels of Mons*. His original story had not mentioned angels. As a writer (he produced some of the best occult stories in the language), he was certainly susceptible to elements of the supernatural, but he loathed formal religion. As he wrote in his introduction to *The Angels of Mons*: 'Well, I have long maintained that on the whole the average church, considered as a house of preaching, is a much more poisonous place than the average tavern.' Nonetheless, the Mons Angels lodged in the public mind as an enduring war legend, even if the troops serving in the British Army always had their doubts about receiving angelic reinforcements. When I was doing my national service in 1960, at a camp in Aldershot called 'Mons', one of the favourite complaints about something that had gone wrong was that it was 'the biggest fuck-up' ('cock-up', if ladies or other sensitive souls were present) 'since Mons'.

But – and this is a mysterious thing – the English have always glorified cock-ups that testify to their indomitable pluck. What, other than a cock-up, was Dunkirk? (See 'Take to the Boats!' below.) Or that bridge-too-far cock-up, Arnhem?

Let's warm the cockles of the Brexiteer's heart with a full recitation of the poem on the greatest, most gloriously versified cock-up of all: 'The Charge of the Light Brigade' by Alfred, Lord Tennyson:

> Half a league, half a league,
> Half a league onward,
> All in the valley of Death
> Rode the six hundred.

'Forward, the Light Brigade!
Charge for the guns!' he said.
Into the valley of Death
Rode the six hundred.

'Forward, the Light Brigade!'
Was there a man dismayed?
Not though the soldier knew
Someone had blundered.
Theirs not to make reply,
Theirs not to reason why,
Theirs but to do and die.
Into the valley of Death
Rode the six hundred.

Cannon to right of them,
Cannon to left of them,
Cannon in front of them
Volleyed and thundered;
Stormed at with shot and shell,
Boldly they rode and well,
Into the jaws of Death,
Into the mouth of hell
Rode the six hundred.

Flashed all their sabres bare,
Flashed as they turned in air
Sabring the gunners there,
Charging an army, while
All the world wondered.
Plunged in the battery-smoke
Right through the line they broke;
Cossack and Russian

Reeled from the sabre ſtroke
Shattered and sundered.
Then they rode back, but not
Not the six hundred.

Cannon to right of them,
Cannon to left of them,
Cannon behind them
Volleyed and thundered;
Stormed at with shot and shell,
While horse and hero fell.
They that had fought so well
Came through the jaws of Death,
Back from the mouth of hell,
All that was left of them,
Left of six hundred.

When can their glory fade?
O the wild charge they made!
All the world wondered.
Honour the charge they made!
Honour the Light Brigade,
Noble six hundred!

One is so carried away that one forgives the appalling rhyme
'thundered/hundred'. It is hard to put one's finger squarely
on why, but one feels this work should be high in the Brexit
hymnal. It expresses, as did *The Battle of Maldon*, something
glorious in English heroic failure. Say not the carnage naught
availeth.

Flashman

Tennyson's anthem to glorious military futility leads, ineluctably, to George MacDonald Fraser, creator of Harry Flashman, the greatest (staunchly English) anti-hero in modern fiction. Flashy's *Who's Who* entry, a comic masterpiece in its own right, prefaces every novel in the series. He is loaded with honour and military rank. He also has the 'Legion of Honour; Order of Maria Theresa, Austria; Order of the Elephant, Denmark (temporary); u.s. Medal of Honor; San Serafino Order of Purity and Truth'. It goes on, down to his being a director (ho hum) of the British Opium Trading Co. and honorary president of the Mission for Reclamation of Reduced Females (he's reduced more than his share), and the fact that the *Wisden Almanack* records him as being the first bowler to have achieved a hat-trick at Lord's.

Fraser, who saw front-line action in the Second World War, had little time for the folderol of the British Empire, but nonetheless believed in what it fundamentally 'stood for'. It was bollocks (as Orwell would say), but there was something very worthwhile behind it all. Orwell, if one reads a work such as *The Lion and the Unicorn* (1941), was of much the same mind, and so was Enoch Powell. So, by and large, is UKIP. It is nice to record that Fraser was awarded an OBE (Officer of the Order of the British Empire); Powell merely received the lower rank MBE (Member of the Order of the British Empire).

Flashman's career as an utter bounder begins at Rugby, the educational pioneer, under Dr Thomas Arnold, of the country's public school ethos (immortalized in Thomas Hughes's novel *Tom Brown's Schooldays* of 1857). The public school was the backbone of empire, supplying the corps of generals and high administrators that kept the enterprise going. Flashy is singularly lacking in backbone, but, when push comes to shove, he does his bit. He's English, for God's sake.

In the first instalment of the *Flashman* (1969) sequence, Fraser turns *Tom Brown's Schooldays* arse-over-tip (as Flashy would say) by making a hero out of the bully who roasts Hughes's hero over the dormitory fire to 'persuade' him to hand over his lottery ticket.[98] Flashman is subsequently expelled by Arnold after being brought back on a shutter, dead drunk, from the local gin palace, having delayed to impregnate the barmaid and put his drinks on the slate.

Perversely (or inversely), in Fraser's extension of the subplot, Flashy goes on to great glory: he is ennobled, promoted and decorated – but, of course, remains at heart (a black organ) the same unregenerate cad, bounder, lecher, knave, chancer and coward who bullied, basted and (we are free to presume) buggered the lower-form boys at Rugby.

In Fraser's version, Flashman is nonetheless lovable with it. And, when he has to be, oddly heroic. After reading the twelve-volume saga, one ends up thinking, 'Stap me – one wouldn't leave one's wife alone with him, but, all in all, he's a damned fine Englishman. Rather be up the Khyber with him than with that puling priggish bore Brown.'

In the first of the books, Flashy is indeed up the Khyber (another army proverb for military failure), in the disastrous First Afghan War. He wins a Victoria Cross – although 'wins' is perhaps the wrong word, and VD is more his style than VC. It's worth noting that we never sorted things out in Afghanistan – still up the Khyber.

The finest of the series (for my money) is *Flashman at the Charge*, the fourth instalment of the rogue's progress. It is also, I would suggest, the most appropriate for Brexiteers to read, if they haven't already. The novel ponders, as did Tennyson, that 'magnificent but not war' display of essential English grit (the

John Wayne movie *True Grit* recycles, at its climax, the Charge of the Light Brigade).

Flashman at the Charge covers the period 1854–5. The hero, born in 1822, is now in his caddish prime. A captain in the cavalry, he is promoted to colonel during the course of the book. The vc 'won' in the Khyber has helped immensely. The novel opens briskly: 'The moment after Lew Nolan wheeled his horse away and disappeared over the edge of the escarpment with Raglan's message tucked in his gauntlet, I knew I was for it.' Into the valley of Death, and all that.

From the imminent charge of the glorious six hundred, there follows a long flashback to London in the period leading up to the Crimean War. Flashy has been angling for a cushy berth in ordnance, where the bullets don't fly but are stored safely in their ammo boxes. He was earlier dismissed from Lord Cardigan's Hussars for having married (a paternal shotgun at the nape of his neck) a Scottish tradesman's daughter called Elspeth, who now has a son (whose? She's as much of a rogue as her husband). Much against his self-preserving instincts, Flashy finds himself ordered by Lord Raglan back to active duties. Fleshpots farewell.

In a state of pure funk, and purely by accident, farting uncontrollably from an injudicious meal the night before, he finds himself galloping in the Charge of the Light Brigade by Cardigan's side. 'It was bloody lunacy from the start, and bloody carnage, too,' is his old soldier's un-Tennysonian verdict, although he kills his share of Russians. Ever the survivor, he is taken prisoner and, as a high-ranking enemy officer, billeted with a Tsarist nobleman, whose daughter he inevitably rogers. In a mad sledge ride he later throws her overboard to stave off a pack of pursuing wolves – Flashy always dumps his ladies in style. Ethics don't always come into it.

He subsequently teams up with his old schoolmate (and dormitory victim) from his Rugby days, 'Scud' East, who is also a prisoner of war. They come across a Russian plot to invade India through the Khyber Pass, and resolve to escape and warn the British authorities (or at least, Scud resolves; Flashy would be happy to remain in his comfortable Russian berth until the pointless war is over).

Many adventures ensue, culminating in our anti-hero – disguised as a tribesman – leading an Afghan rebellion against the Russians, transformed into a bloody warrior ('utterly against nature, instinct and judgement') by a potion of hashish, administered by his exotic Mongol princess lover, who perceives that his spine is less firm than his cock. More glory awaits on his return to a grateful queen and nation, proud to have such warriors as Colonel Harold Flashman, vc, protecting – nay, enlarging – an empire on which the sun never sets.

Flashman at the Charge was serialized, in full, in *Playboy*. Flashy would have loved that.

THERE WILL ALAS be no more Flashy for us. Shortly before his death in 2008, Fraser published his last testament as an uncompromisingly titled article in the *Daily Mail*, a congenial organ politically, as was made clear.[99] It opens:

> When 30 years ago I resurrected Flashman ... political correctness hadn't been heard of, and no exception was taken to my adopted hero's character, behaviour, attitude to women and subject races (indeed, any races, including his own) and general awfulness.
>
> On the contrary, it soon became evident that these were his main attractions. He was politically incorrect with a vengeance.
>
> Through the Seventies and Eighties I led him on his disgraceful way, toadying, lying, cheating, running away, treating women as chattels, abusing inferiors of all

colours, with only one redeeming virtue – the unsparing honesty with which he admitted to his faults, and even gloried in them.

And no one minded, or if they did, they didn't tell me. In all the many thousands of readers' letters I received, not one objected.

In the Nineties, a change began to take place. Reviewers and interviewers started describing Flashman (and me) as politically incorrect, which we are, though by no means in the same way.

Thundering on in this way for several thousand words, Fraser excoriated the moral rot behind PC, working himself up to a full-bore diatribe against its

selective distortions of history . . . denigrating Britain's past with such propaganda as hopelessly unbalanced accounts of the slave trade, laying all the blame on the white races, but carefully censoring the truth that not a slave could have come out of Africa without the active assistance of black slavers, and that the trade was only finally suppressed by the Royal Navy virtually single-handed . . .

That PC should have become acceptable in Britain is a glaring symptom of the country's decline . . .

Other lands have known what seem to be greater upheavals, the result of wars and revolutions, but these do not compare with the experience of a country which passed in less than a lifetime from being the mightiest empire in history, governing a quarter of mankind, to being a feeble little offshore island whose so-called leaders have lost the will and the courage, indeed the ability, to govern at all . . .

My generation has seen the decay of ordinary morality, standards of decency, sportsmanship, politeness, respect for the law, family values, politics and education and religion, the very character of the British ...

We have had the two worst Prime Ministers in our history – Edward Heath (who dragooned us into the Common Market) and Tony Blair. The harm these two have done to Britain is incalculable and almost certainly irreparable.

Perhaps, after 23 June 2016, it may not be beyond repair. Fraser did not live to vote, but he left something more trenchant: a battle cry.

Goldfinger

A strong contender for the 'everyone's favourite Bond' prize, *Goldfinger* was the work that converted into the Bond series' most inventive film adaptation five years later. There is no need to stress Ian Fleming's Englishness (why was he never knighted?) or the defiant Englishness (with a bracing touch of Scot) of 'Bond, James Bond'.[100] Agent 007 (licensed to kill) is the living assertion that quaint little England, even stripped of the empire that once made it Great Britain, can punch, assassinate and copulate well above its diminished weight.

At every point, Bond fiction reassures the English reader that England matters. England has style and sexuality (women fall for Bond like ninepins, many more than nine of them). His adventures and conquests are, not to mince words, a massive male compensation fantasy. *Goldfinger* was given to the world only three years after the Suez debacle, which demonstrated that Britain was nothing more than a spear-carrier, no longer a superpower, on the international stage. Bond is, however, super-powered.

The novel opens in Mexico, with Bond effortlessly rubbing out a Mexican hitman employed by the Capunga drug cartel, which Bond has just mightily inconvenienced. The 'dago' killer carries a knife – all Mexicans do. Orwell made the point in his study of boys' literature, just as Scotsmen wear nothing under their kilts. As Shakespeare says in *The Winter's Tale*, men yearn to be 'boys eternal'. One could draw that conclusion from the Bond tales.

The story is simple and, as usual, preposterous. On a transit few days in Miami, Bond clashes over the card table with Auric Goldfinger. In 1959 there was a looser grip than there is now on casual racism in fiction. 'Is Goldfinger Jewish?' it is repeatedly asked in the novel. A little smear of anti-Semitism is streaked across the narrative, only to be erased – but not entirely. 'You won't believe it,' it's later asserted, 'but he's a Britisher. Domiciled in Nassau. You'd think he'd be a Jew from the name, but he doesn't look it,' Bond is informed.[101] Bond unconvincingly deduces from the available evidence that Auric Goldfinger is, aboriginally, a 'Balt' – which makes him sound like a deep-sea fish. But he is, incontrovertibly, vaguely European. And, to be Podsnappish, 'not English', with knobs on.

Goldfinger keeps a Korean retinue, ostensibly because he likes their golden skin. But the West, particularly America and Britain, was still smarting from near defeat in the 1953 war on the Korean peninsula. Fleming feels able to unload a mass of xenophobic slander in the novel: 'The Koreans', Goldfinger cheerfully informs Bond, are 'the cruellest, most ruthless people in the world.' Their favourite food is the domestic cat; their only pleasure in life inflicting unspeakable sexual perversions on white women.

Oddjob, Auric Goldfinger's Jeeves, is a particularly formidable specimen of his race – the Yellow Peril incarnate. Unlike Wodehouse's gentleman's gentleman, Oddjob is a fifth-dan black-belt karate (Fleming's millions-selling novel introduced the k-word into British and American cultural awareness, along with Korean feline appetites).

What is Goldfinger's mission? It is simply stated: to acquire the world's greatest hoard of gold – and, presumably, goldfinger it at will; he surely won't be able to do anything with it, just like Tolkien's Smaug (another vaguely anti-Semitic stereotype), who can do nothing but sleep on his mountain of the stuff. Uncomfortable, one would have thought. The novel contains a long disquisition by the chief of the Bank of England, who tells Bond that Goldfinger's illegal siphoning of gold out of the country (via a chain of pawn shops) will rob Britain of what remains of its international power. It will be the world's only banana republic where bananas don't grow, just turnips.

In the late 1950s the pound sterling was, alongside the dollar, a 'reserve currency' – foundational to the world economic order. The pound's reliability depended on the country having sufficient gold to redeem its paper promises.

In addition to his financial machinations, Goldfinger is also, Bond's control, 'M', suspects, a Russian SMERSH operative, financing that sinister agency's activities with his loot – the better to weaken England and get at its loot. SMERSH, too, is keen on destroying Britain.

The SMERSH connection, if one thinks about it (but who thinks while reading about Bond's doings?), doesn't ring true. If Goldfinger is an agent, he can hardly be called a secret agent. His clothes, his hair, his car and even his cat (Oddjob's snack-in-waiting) are golden-hued, gold-plated or golden-dyed. His trademark kink is to daub his once-a-month hired escorts with gold paint before having sex with them.

The novel's action moves to Switzerland, the entrepôt for Goldfinger's smuggling. Those damned gnomes (in the early 1960s, the British press saw Switzerland, and its financiers, as inveterate enemies of the pound sterling). Bond discovers that Goldfinger's car has, under its vulgar gold paint, pure gold panels. The metal is later smuggled – via unconscious passenger buttock, in the form of covered airliner seats – to India, where it is sold at huge profit on the black market. India is as greedy for the precious metal as is Goldfinger, cunning devil.

At this point, the narrative goes further down the rabbit hole into Wonderland. Escaping from being divided in half by a circular saw starting its cut with his genitals (in the film it is a laser), Bond improbably contrives to get himself recruited into Goldfinger's entourage. A titanic heist is being planned, whereby Goldfinger – using the combined forces of America's two leading crime families (with the improbably named 'Spangled Mob' at their head) and Pussy Galore's crew of air pilot(ess) lesbian commandos – intends to rob Fort Knox. He will poison the water supply, then simply walk in past the dead defenders and help himself. A fleet of hired trucks will carry away the thousands of tons of gold to some port where the customs authorities will conveniently not have heard about the biggest bullion robbery in American history.

Bond goes to work. He seduces Pussy and saves her for heterosexuality. He also saves America's gold reserve by getting a message out to his old CIA buddy Felix Leiter. There is a final encounter on the plane on which Goldfinger and Oddjob are making their escape. Bond strangles the master criminal and shoots out a window, through which Goldfinger's Korean sidekick (his karate sidekicks don't help him now) is sucked out like so much golden toothpaste. Pussy, as she and Bond find themselves afloat in a rescue raft, will receive a gentler cruelty from 007: 'His right hand came slowly up her firm, muscled thighs, over the flat plane of the stomach to the right breast. Its point was hard with desire. He said softly, "Now." His mouth came ruthlessly down on hers.' What Fleming calls (outrageously) the 'sweet tang of rape' is in prospect. More importantly, Bond has saved England. Hip hip. (The film improves on the book's absurd Fort Knox caper by having Goldfinger irradiate the American gold with a Chinese nuclear device, thus driving up the value of his lesser hoard.)

What should interest today's readers, vis-à-vis Brexit, is the key episode in the novel: an extended game of golf between Bond and Goldfinger. It takes place on St Mark's links (clearly identifiable as the Royal St George's course in Sandwich, Kent). The two men, both handicapped nine, are evenly pitted. The stake they decide to play for (at Bond's instigation) is high: £20,000.

Golf clubs were, in the late 1950s, one of the most obstinate bastions of English prejudice. No one without a good school tie, no women, few Jews, no Balts (probably) were welcome. One black ball was enough to keep the nineteenth hole exclusive. Members of a good club were upper. The professionals and caddies – like non-commissioned ranks in the army – knew their place in a well-run golf club, assuming they wanted to keep their place. For Old Englanders, the 'club' was a home from home. The contest between Goldfinger and Bond is reminiscent of the Battle of Maldon – not mud, but manicured turf and bunkers. It is, of course, England the two men are competing for, with their clubs (weaponry that goes back to the Stone Age).

Fleming was a bit shaky about some things (Mexican drug criminals and the structure of Cosa Nostra, for example), but he surely knew his golf. Consider the following:

At the seventh, five hundred yards [Bond's] good drives and Goldfinger's immaculate second lay fifty yards short of the green. Bond took his brassie. Now for the equal-izer! But he hit from the top, his club head came too far ahead of the hands and the smothered ball shot into one of the right hand bunkers. Not a good lie, but he muſt put it on the green. Bond took a dangerous seven and failed to get it out. Goldfinger got his five. Two down. They halved the short eighth in three. At the ninth Bond, determined to turn only one down, again tried too much off a poor lie. Goldfinger got his four to Bond's five. Three down at the turn! Not too good.

His caddy, Hawker, whispers to Bond that Goldfinger is cheat-ing. Cunningly. Both men cheat, in fact: they are playing a higher game that is not golf. And the stake is England. But Bond cheats more cunningly, as, in between, he plays more 'honest' golf.

What, then, should the Brexiteer make of *Goldfinger*? In the above summary I have heightened some things that jar for the reader of today. But the novel, in the context of a country still wincing from the Suez catastrophe, expresses a confidence in England and its larger self, Great Britain. It is something that cannot be 'amalgamated', whether into the Atlantic community (Bond is forever a step ahead of the doltish CIA) or the EU. Gold-hungry Balts, tax-hungry Brussels – what's the difference?

The Poison Cabinet

There is a dark fringe whose literature is kept discreetly off the shelf, in a literary version of the poison cabinet. Does the well-versed Kipper want to open it and sniff its mephitic contents? A representative *livre noir* is that novel of the interna-tional far right (a declared favourite of Marine Le Pen and of her father, Jean-Marie Le Pen), Jean Raspail's *The Camp of the Saints*.

The novel was first published in 1973 in France. No British publisher, to their collective credit, has cared to take it on. In America, publication was sponsored in 1985 by the ultra-right, anti-immigration Laurel Foundation, under whose aegis the translation now sells, apparently, like hot cakes. It is also available these days from Amazon.

The Camp of the Saints has been adopted in the USA by the so-called alt-right as a text expressing what they stand for. It is routinely applauded in the Breitbart News Network, whose founding spirit was Steve Bannon, erstwhile colleague of – and manifestly a strong ideological influence on – President Donald Trump.[102] 'It's not a migration,' Bannon said of Europe's accepting refugees in January 2016. 'It's really an invasion. I call it the Camp of the Saints.' Slap that across the back cover of the Laurel edition.

A similarly minded *Breitbart* article in 2015 declared:

> fast forward 40 years, to 2014: Europe is under demographic siege, and so is America. Raspail's nightmare scenario is coming to pass on both continents. Indeed, the current scenes along the U.S.–Mexican border seem like a sequel to *The Camp of the Saints*.[103]

Raspail's novel foretells an imminent 'swamping' of Europe by disgusting illegals from the 'orient'. Forget passports or border controls: they just hijack tankers and come, an armada of subcontinental sub-humanity, an alien tsunami. Their behaviour en route forecasts what Europe can expect from these new Europeans once they make land: 'Everywhere, rivers of sperm. Streaming over bodies, oozing between breasts and buttocks and thighs and lips and fingers ... a welter of dung and debauch.' It's not the healthiest form of travel, but 800,000 make it to the south coast of France. In 1973 that seemed a huge number of uninvited immigrant bodies. Margaret Thatcher, one may recall, thought 100,000 would 'swamp' the UK; in the last years of EU membership, Britain was running at three times that – and coping well, many would have claimed. Angela Merkel let into Germany a million of the kinds of refugee Raspail disgustingly slanders. The country was not overrun, although there were hiccups.

In Raspail's book, Europe is so enervated by neo-liberalism and postcolonial guilt and depopulated by 'family planning' – he is ultra-Catholic – that the alien tide laps over the continent, 'with a stench of latrines', like effluent from a broken sewage pipe. A small resistance band, the 'Saints', is liquidated – by the French government. The immigrants come, they settle, they rape, they steal. Above all, they multiply. Raspail calls it 'the Calcutta solution': genocide by the simple technique of the cuckoo in some other bird's nest. Europe becomes a heart of darkness. The title comes from the Book of Revelation, and indeed the novel's vision is apocalyptic. France will never rise again.

Raspail's loathsome novel has over the years achieved something like respectability. The author has a website and has been called 'the Frantz Fanon of the White Race'. *The Camp of the Saints* articulates, in its obscene extremity, a Western nightmare fashionable, in milder versions, among neoconservatives. Civilizations won't 'clash', as Samuel Huntington prophesied; the developed world (and, in the Middle East, Israel) will simply be 'outspawned' (Raspail's terminology) into racial extinction.

This thesis does have spurious, sub-Malthusian demography behind it. 'Yes,' the last paragraph of Salman Rushdie's *Midnight's Children* (1981) prophesies, 'they will trample me underfoot, the numbers marching one two three, four hundred million five hundred six.' The population of India, 35 years after Rushdie wrote those words, was 1.3 billion or more. And twenty years on? Where will those still more millions go? Raspail knows: the Côte d'Azur. The whole vision of *The Camp of the Saints* is disgustingly wrong, and it does great mischief. It does not help that the novel is not at all badly written.

Raspail's brutally xenophobic vision of the future is given a subtle revisioning in Michel Houellebecq's book *Submission* (2015), in which France is too nerveless to resist a cancerous Muslim takeover from within (again enabled by the ability of 'aliens' to outbreed natives). The *résistance* is no more. Where Hitler failed, the imams succeed; France is totally Islamicized. To use a dirty word from the Second World War, the country 'collaborates', since it is less costly than fighting. Houellebecq's novel rests on a bleak contention, that submission is the better part of valour.

UKIP has an equivocal relationship with *The Camp of the Saints*. On 26 April 2015 the party's affiliated (but not party-controlled) web-paper *Ukip Daily* ran an article by Robert Henderson, entitled 'See Mass Migration for What It Is – Invasion'. It opened:

> The French writer Jean Raspail's *Camp of the Saints* describes a situation not unlike that of the present exodus from North Africa and the Middle East. In Raspail's book the invasion is by large ships crammed with Third World migrants coming to Europe where the ships are beached and the migrants flood into Europe, a Europe which has lost the will to resist because of decades of politically correct internationalist propaganda. Europe and eventually the entire developed world falls to the invasion of the Third World hordes who are armed only with their misery and the Pavlovian response of First World populations who have lost the will to resist because they have been brainwashed by the multicultural propaganda. This is the scenario that is now being acted

out in the Mediterranean, but with, in the main, small boats, rather than large ones carrying the migrants.

The ſtark truth is that mass immigration is invasion resulting in the effeꞔive colonisation of parts of the invaded country because immigrants from a similar background have a pronounced tendency to congregate in the same area. Any other description of mass immigration is wilfully dishoneſt. It is as reasonable for a people to resiſt invasion by mass immigration as it is to [resiſt] an invasion by an armed invader.

Fighting talk. And nonsense.

The Camp of the Saints is French fiction, and therefore outside the orbit of this book. But the Good Brexiteer should be aware of Raspail's polemic, examine it and pass it by with a shudder of disgust. It perverts the common-ground decencies that, love it or loathe it, UKIP can reasonably claim to embody.

Lost Englands

'There'll always be an England,' sang Vera Lynn to a nervous country in 1939. No there won't, says history (and, obliquely, the Sex Pistols, who merrily punked the song up in their stage appearances). Fiction has pictured the end of England in various ways: nostalgic (see below, 'Virginia Woolf's Farewell to England (and the World)'); comic (see '*The Queen and I*'); Gothic (see '*London Fields*'); and satiric (see '*England, England*'). The best-known apocalyptic vision of England gone forever (leaving a boot stamping on the English face) is Orwell's, in *Nineteen Eighty-four*. What was once England is now Airstrip One – Oceania's aircraft carrier. The English are no more, and the governing (forever) Party, in the interest of suppressing thoughtcrime, is shrinking the richness of the English tongue into a few hundred vocables of 'Newspeak'. Verbal Lego. The oed's many, ever-growing volumes will be shrunk into something as thick as the Highway Code. Literature? The canon will be trash mechanically produced by Pornosec.

Identifying what UKIP and Brexit stand for is difficult, and indeed one wonders if they always know themselves. But one motive, clearly enough, is saving old England, restoring the country to what it was before it melted into the supranational Grimpen Mire of 'Europe'. If UKIP wanted an anthem, 'There'll Always Be an England', as sung by Vera, the people's favourite, would serve. Some of England's best novelists choose to disagree about the everlastingness of our country – as it once was. The disagreement throws sidelights on what Brexit is all about.

Virginia Woolf's Farewell to England (and the World)

Woolf wrote her last novel in the firm belief that England – the England she loved, almost despite herself – was to be destroyed in mere weeks. She expressed that conviction, and with it the expectation that she would not let herself live to see it, in her last novel.

Between the Acts (1941) was published posthumously, unrevised (something the literary perfectionist in Woolf would have resented), a few months after her suicide. One cannot read it without wondering, poignantly, how many interesting lines of English fiction went to the grave with the writer, whose art was observably at a transitional stage in its evolution.

The flat in which Woolf wrote most of the novel, in Bloomsbury (which was her intellectual as well as her physical home), had been destroyed by bombs in the Blitz. In the early chapters of *Between the Acts*, characters are constantly looking up at the skies, at birds they cannot always identify ('Is it a nightingale?'). The whole population of Britain (I was one) spent a lot of time looking skywards – not for nightingales but for Dorniers, Messerschmitts, planes we could not identify ('Is it ours or theirs?').

Woolf finished her novel in the Sussex countryside, near the river where she would very soon drown herself, and near the English Channel, over which, it was plausibly feared in spring 1941, the Germans would cross and do to England what they were doing to France. The action of the novel takes place over one day in high summer of 1939. War broke out in the first week of September, as the harvest was being brought in. 'Between the acts' is a direct allusion to the annual village historical pageant at the centre of the action. But it is also a hint at the tense interval between the two great historical acts of war and peace, in Tolstoy's titular phrase. A 'phoney' war, it was called in late 1939 and early 1940.

Woolf's first chapter begins: 'It was a summer's night and they were talking, in the big room with the windows open to the garden, about the cesspool. The county council had promised to bring water to the village, but they hadn't.' Life, as they say, goes on – as do complaints about the council. The setting is a traditional one for 'condition of England' fiction: a country house. The action takes place in Pointz Hall, seat of the Oliver family. The Olivers are headed by the patriarch Bartholomew ('of the Indian Civil Service, retired') and his widowed sister Lucy Swithin. The younger (not very) generation comprises Isa and Giles Oliver (he is 'something in the City') and their son George. The Olivers' marriage is going badly, and they bicker. Isa is poetic and yearns, Madame Bovary-style, for a larger emotional life, with a partner more Byronic than Giles. She has her eye on a local philanderer, who is himself married.

The big day goes badly. Lunch guests, the florid Mrs Manresa (on whom Giles's roving eye has settled) and the effete William Dodge (a 'degenerate' – that is to say, gay), prove to be awkward company. The afternoon highlight is the 'pageant', a mockery of English history through the ages. It is presented by the busy-bodying Miss La Trobe, and flops. 'Her gift', she sadly concludes, 'meant nothing. If they had understood her meaning; if they had known their parts; if the pearls had been real and the funds illimitable – it would have been a better gift. Now it had gone to join the others. "A failure," she groaned.'

The pageant opens with 'Merry England', then moves on to Elizabethan glory, the Industrial Revolution, Empire and . . . what next? Deutschland über Alles?[104] The novel sidesteps that all-important question, ending at bedtime with Isa and Giles about to fight, copulate and sleep. From their grudging embrace, 'another life might be born. But first they must fight, as the dog fox fights with the vixen, in the heart of darkness, in the fields of night.'

During the war, the Woolfs (Virginia's husband, Leonard, was Jewish and left-wing) were on the Gestapo extermination list. He, like her, had plans for suicide (in his case, from carbon monoxide poisoning in the locked garage – he planned to do it *à deux* with the writer Stephen Spender), when the Germans invaded. Virginia preferred the 'cleaner' method of asphyxiation by fresh river water. Why live, her last novel asks, when England is doomed? It wasn't, thank the Lord (who loves us; see above).

Postscript: *SS-GB*

Woolf could not face the prospect of Germany Germanizing England. Death was preferable. And so would Leonard Woolf have killed himself, as planned, if the Germans had indeed arrived. Science fiction, however, speculates inventively on this scenario. Philip K. Dick did not invent AU/SF (alternative universe science fiction), but he popularized it with his novel *The Man in the High Castle* (1962), which fantasizes a world in which Germany and Japan won the Second World War and have, as conquerors, brutally disunited the USA into two separate fiefdoms.

Relevant here, however, is the British AU/SF fantasia *SS-GB* (1978) by Len Deighton, who started writing it immediately after Britain entered the Common Market (as it then was). *SS-GB* led the hardback lists in 1978, and the paperback lists in 1980. It was big.

The novel portrays an England of 1941 whose empire has imploded like a white dwarf. In February that year British Command surrenders abjectly to the Nazis. Churchill has been executed, the King is in the Tower and the German SS runs Whitehall. For nine months Britain has been occupied – a Blitzed, depressed and dingy Vichy.

The plot of *SS-GB* is that of a murder hunt by Scotland Yard (business as usual – the wartime shop slogan, even with all the windows blown out), but that eventually becomes mixed with the 'secret weapon', the atom bomb, and British Jewish nuclear scientists who know how to make it. The Germans want the bomb, but not the Jews. If America gets there first Britain may be saved – or annihilated, when the bomb drops in nuclear interchange.

Deighton artfully, as the structuralists say, makes London 'strange', but still, under the veneer of German conquest, it remains familiar 1940s London (I remember it well):

> In the air there was the green, sooty fog typical of those that London suffered, but the rider [of the motorcycle, carrying the detective hero] did not slacken speed. A Gendarmerie foot patrol was marching through the

Victoria railway station forecourt but they ignored the ss motorcycle. The fog was worse as they neared the river, and Douglas caught the ugly smell of it. After Vauxhall Bridge, the motor-cyclist turned right, into a street of squat little houses and high brick walls, and advertisement hoardings, upon which appeals for volunteers to work in German factories, announcements about rationing and a freshly pasted German–Soviet Friendship Week poster shone rain-wet through the fog.

It resonates historically that Deighton's SF scenario, fantasizing a Gothic domination of England by Germany, was published as the UK took the plunge: Brentry. Opponents such as Enoch Powell declared that such a move would ultimately become subjugation by the *BRD-GB*, the Brexit nightmare.

Also significant is the fact that *SS-GB* was revived, as a high-budget five-part BBC TV serial, in February and March 2017, the moment of Brexit. The series was commissioned, conceived and in early production from 2014, reaching completion as the UK was making its epic decision in June 2016.

This bracket (1978/2017) rubs a sore point: the sense that in joining the Common Market, later the European Community and European Union, the UK had indeed been abasing itself to the Union's dominant member, Germany, now vastly enlarged in *Raum und Kraft* by unification. Wikipedia records that the series received 'highly positive reviews'. A zeitgeist thing, one would like to think.

The Queen and I

Sue Townsend, the creator of that most misunderstood of
teenage heroes, Adrian Mole, published her monarchic skit
The Queen and I in 1992. It was a grim year. On 'Black Wednesday'
(16 September), the UK had been forced out of the European
Exchange Rate Mechanism, plunging the pound to new depths.
It was a fore-tremor. Institutions that held up the realm were
shaking.

Until the 1960s, it was very nearly treason to depict the
reigning monarch on stage, in film or in literature. After that lib-
erating decade, the world of entertainment became more daring,
no longer fearful of the Tower, nose-slitting or being whipped
through London at the tail of a cart. The Lord Chamberlain,
who weighed so heavily on Shakespeare (so much so that he
never dared to set a comedy in London), was a dead letter. Let
lese-majesty thrive, but not, like the French, by guillotine.

Prince Charles was elsewhere made to play a part in a Tom
Clancy novel, and, horror of horrors, the monarch herself was
spoofed by a professional lookalike in the slapstick film *The
Naked Gun* (1988; luckily, by then cinemas were no longer
required to end the evening with 'The Queen', with the whole
audience standing to attention).

No jester was jollier, or friendlier (in her way) about the
'Royals', than Townsend. And no popular novelist of the time
started life lower down the class ladder. She was that rarity
among novelists: *echt* working class, born one of the post-war
'bulge' – the population explosion that brought the country's
resources to rupture point (now retiring 'baby boomers', still
rupturing away).

Townsend was the daughter of a postman, brought up in a
'prefab', one of the rabbit hutches built for the heroes who won

the war. The eldest of five sisters ('very Chekhovian,' she said), she had low expectations of life. Young Susan failed the eleven-plus and attended a 'secondary modern' a stone's throw away from the grammar school she did not get into. She left school at fifteen, at the earliest possible moment, married too soon and unwisely, and had three children (nothing Chekhovian about that), all the while reading Penguin Books ('my university') and cultivating her God-given talent as a 'secret writer' (she kept her manuscripts in a cupboard with the brooms). Then came Adrian and bestselling success.

The Queen and I takes place after a bloodless revolution, in which the Socialists have taken over. The House of Windsor finds itself rehomed in a Midlands council house in Hellebore Close (nicknamed 'Hell Close'). It's a 'learning experience':

> 'Mr Barker, there is no mention of dogs here,' said the Queen.
> 'One per family,' said Jack.
> 'Horses?' asked Charles.
> 'Would you keep a horse in a council house garden?'
> 'No. Quite. One wasn't thinking.'
> 'Clothes aren't on the list,' said Diana, shyly.
> 'You won't be needing much. Just the bare essentials. You won't be making personal appearances, will you?'
> Princess Anne rose and stood next to her father. 'Thank God for that! At least something good has come out of this bloody shambles. Are you all right, Pa?'

The monarch, along with her loyal 'dorgi' (corgi doggy) Harris, ingeniously makes do on her state pension – 'Mrs Windsor' is now a welfare queen. Charles chats all day to his garden plants, and Diana misconducts herself with some racy fellows up the street. When the Queen Mum dies (she was going strong at the time the novel was published), Hellebore comes together to give her a mini state funeral. At the end of the narrative, what's left of England is bought by Japan – cut-price.[105]

The Children of Men

P. D. JAMES's novel *The Children of Men* (1992), a striking departure from her detective fiction, was adapted into a film in 2006. The author approved of the adaptation, despite the fact that it altered in some ways her analysis of what has gone wrong with England. The plot of both versions recalls Margaret Atwood's *The Handmaid's Tale*.

The dominant voice in the narrative is that of Theo Faron, an Oxford don, chronicling the extinction of his species in his diary in 2021 (or, in the film version, 2027). What he records is a world that has lost its genetic potency – it no longer procreates. Male sperm is at fault. By 1995, the 'Year Omega', it was as unfit for purpose as curdled mayonnaise. Since that year no children have been born, nor will they ever be, apparently. A bleak newspaper report announces: 'Early this morning, 1 January 2021, three minutes after midnight, the last human being to be born on earth was killed in a pub brawl in a suburb of Buenos Aires, aged twenty-five years, two months and twelve days.' The last generation to be born – the 'Omegans'– are wanton sybarites. 'Without hope of a future,' the novel asserts, 'man becomes a beast.' The population at large is subjected to regular medical inspections that merely confirm the worst. Household pets – from kittens to budgerigars – have grotesquely displaced parental love lavished on them. What little vitality eunuch England possesses has been sucked in from abroad, vampirically, by mass immigration. State-enforced euthanasia at sixty (by mass drowning) is enforced. Democracy, without a demographic foundation, collapses.

The country is run, despotically, by a Warden, Xan Lyppiatt (a relative of Theo's). The plot develops when Theo becomes involved with an underground group, the Five Fishes (named after the biblical miracle), who plan counter-revolution and the re-establishment of democracy. Their resistance becomes violent and the climax comes when one of their number, a woman called Julian, becomes pregnant. The narrative ends with a duel between Theo and Xan in the woods where Julian's baby is being born. The good guy wins, and there may be hope for the future, although the novel makes no promises.[106]

London Fields

There are those who say that *London Fields* is Martin Amis's best novel, and those who say that, closing in on seventy, he has not yet written his best novel. I find I can hold both opinions simultaneously – particularly after reading this end-of-England work.

London Fields is a novel much concerned with dying. 'Death is killing me,' the hero says at one point. Amis's word-play consistently has deeper meaning; here that England is dying, Earth is dying, winding down. Our planet, by the novel's doomsday clock, will have expired before the millennium fireworks. It has, over the blazing hot September and October 1999, which the narrative covers, only a few weeks before what is vaguely called the 'Crisis', or 'Totality'. That dire event will occur on 5 November 1999 – as the biggest bonfire night in the history of the planet.

It's not entirely clear what form the rider of the millennial apocalypse will take, nor, oddly, does the novel seem much to care. A colliding asteroid, perhaps, or a new alignment of the sun, itself going through a crisis of solar supergranulation, its evil rays glimmering ominously through 'dead clouds'. A voracious black hole may be swirling towards us, invisibly, sucking in light and soon enough the earth with it.

Presumably believing we might as well go out with a bang, not a whimper, the authorities have scheduled a 'cathartic' exchange of nuclear weaponry. Everything is up in the air. As the sandwich-men used to proclaim, 'the end of the world is nigh.' Very nigh. But, as one of the characters in the novel puts it, 'Life goes on innit.' Briefly.

London Fields, published in September 1989, is the second volume of Amis's so-called London Trilogy.[107] The man who is 'tired of London', boomed Samuel Johnson, is 'tired of life'. Amis would seem to be very tired indeed. His London is the suppurating bubo of a plague planet: a city where the tap water 'has passed at least twice through every granny'. Weather forecasts are so horrific that they are broadcast late at night, after the children have gone to bed. The city is bathed in the corrupt 'afterglow of empire', as poisonous as radioactive half-life: 'This is London; and there are no fields. Only fields of operation and observation, only fields of electromagnetic attraction and repulsion, only fields of hatred and coercion.' 'This also', says Conrad's Marlow in *Heart of Darkness*, looking down the Thames towards the great city, 'has been one of the dark places of the earth.' In *London Fields* it is again a dark place – terminally.

Like D. H. Lawrence (a writer recurrently evoked in *London Fields*), Amis sees the great tree of life, Yggdrasil, as dead to the roots in England. It can never grow again. But unlike Lawrence – who, after the First World War, embarked on his global 'passionate pilgrimage' to discover vitality in places untouched by the catastrophe (largely where men did not wear trousers) – he presents us with nowhere to go in his blighted world. 'Totality' means just that: it's all over. Goodnight.

In 2012 Amis declared that he was leaving England to live in Brooklyn, New York. He misses England, he says, but there is clearly too much missing in England to keep him.

England, England

Contempt for England is an ingredient that is not much encountered in English fiction, but, as the second millennium approached, contempt for England was increasingly invited. What, precisely, was there to celebrate about the country as it now was? Everyone with eyes in their head and a history book on their shelves knew there had been 'decline and fall' – lost an empire and not found a role, and so on.

The Anglo-Saxons were no longer lords of creation, but there was a lingering sense of superiority – our unmatched 'heritage' was, surely, evidence of that. The 'heritage industry' (not to mention the Heritage Lottery Fund) would have been seen, in the years of Great Britain's true greatness, as stuff for Swiftian satire. Julian Barnes duly rose to the challenge in 1998 with *England, England*.

Barnes is a formidably knowing writer, possessed of biting wit, and his title has resonant echoes. D. H. Lawrence and George Orwell wrote works called *England, My England* and 'England your England', respectively. Lawrence's story centres on a market garden, a little Eden, which has supplied a family's needs for generations. The First World War breaks out, and the owner of the garden despairingly throws away his life, fighting for an England he can no longer believe in. The garden ('green and pleasant land') can be preserved no longer; it will be paved over. The story forecasts the theme of Lawrence's last major work, *Lady Chatterley's Lover*, and the Lawrentian *j'accuse* that the great tree of life, Yggdrasil, is dead in England. Alluded to, ironically, in Lawrence's title is the full-throated Victorian anthem by W. E. Henley and its opening: 'What have I done for you, England, my England?/ What is there I would not do, England, my own?' Behind Henley is John of Gaunt's dying speech in *Richard* ii ('This blessed plot, this earth, this realm, this England').

Football fans irreverently recall the war chant at international soccer matches: 'ENGERLAND! ENGERLAND!' Orwell, writing 'England your England' as the German bombers flew overhead, felt that there were indeed English things worth being blown to smithereens for, although his patriotism was more nuanced and dubious than Henley's.

Julian Barnes's *England, England* is, by contrast, a work of full-blooded, virtuoso Anglophobia (England 1990) by England's most distinguished literary Francophile and France's favourite English novelist (not a long list, one suspects). A financier-cum-newspaper-tycoon (he owns *The Times*, the 'paper of record'), Sir Jack Pitman (transparently inspired by the by then seven-years-dead Sir Robert Maxwell), undertakes the creation of a theme-park England (half-size) on the Isle of Wight. Call it (although Barnes was wise not to annoy Disney's fearsome lawyers) 'Englandland'.

Old England can't compete. A new royal couple, including the improbably named Queen Denise, move there to take up residence in a half-size Buckingham Palace. Samuel Johnson splutters ponderously, firing off his 'Sirs!' like musket balls. Battle of Britain pilots lounge in deckchairs waiting for the 'scramble' phone call. Pitman's England joins the EU, diluting its essence, another synthetic construct at the date the novel was written. The tycoon's right-hand woman is fortyish Martha Cochrane, lower-middle-class and ruthlessly ambitious. Together they bring their project to fruition.

The novel is based on the conceit that England has nothing left but its 'heritage', and that Pitman's replica will be more real, more sanitary – above all more saleable – than the real thing. A French theorist is hired to give the venture philosophic sexiness: 'It is important to understand that in the modern world we prefer the replica to the original because it gives us the greater *frisson*. I leave that word in French because I think you understand it well that way.' And, when push comes to shove, the English nation discovers that it really can't be bothered with all the hassle of real things. Pitman's England is 'everything you imagined England to be, but more convenient, cleaner, friendlier, and more efficient'. He is finally brought down by turncoat Martha, who uses incriminating evidence of her employer conducting strange doings in brothels. Having disposed of him, she retires to a hermit existence in 'Anglia' (mainland England), which has reverted to its antique 'Wessex' character. Thomas Hardy's *faux* England, that is.[108]

Take to the Boats!

In August 2017, after attending a preview showing of the film, Nigel Farage tweeted: 'I urge every youngster to go out and watch #Dunkirk.' Farage had evidently seen Christopher Nolan's film on the vast IMAX screen, creating a Sensurround experience. You were not watching the movie, but inside it.

Private Eye had an amusing cover that same week, poking fun at Farage's subtext, showing a crowded landing craft and the caption from a soldier's mouth: 'It's harder to leave than we thought.' Militarily, the Dunkirk evacuation may have been a disaster, but at least the English soldiers were, in a very decisive way, 'leaving' Europe. So were we, after June 2016, with no small boats necessary and little risk the Luftwaffe would strafe us as we departed.

The film does not portray the ignominious flight of 380,000 fighting men from the field of battle as what it was – the biggest cock-up since Mons. Far from it. Little England, in the shape of four hundred little boats (the film, for human interest, concentrates on just one, skippered by Mark Rylance), 'saved the day' (in fact ten days). And so the army lived to fight on.

The general impression Nolan's film gives is that it was a 'damned good show' and that the troops were well organized. It was what military commanders call a 'tactical withdrawal' (never use the word 'retreat'). When the hero of the film, 'Tommy', a plucky private played by Fionn Whitehead, finds himself on the beach, he sees men lined up neatly like so many coconuts at a funfair stall.[109] It would, drawing on my own experience in the ranks, be strictly against military practice to present such close-packed enfilade targets for a raking Spandau machine gun. Easier than coconuts.

Tommy joins the wrong queue – 'this is the Grenadiers, mate,' says the guardsman at the back – and goes off to find his less snooty regimental queue. He is distracted by seeing a wounded comrade, whom he exerts himself to get on to a Royal Navy boat that is just leaving. Way is made for him. On the end of the jetty, supervising embarkation, is Commander Bolton, played by Kenneth Branagh, keeping all shipshape.

Despite the fact that it stands so high in British historical legend, surprisingly few good works of fiction have been written about Dunkirk.[110] By far the best literary treatment, for my money, is that by Ian McEwan in *Atonement* (2001). McEwan always films well, and the director Joe Wright made a superb adaptation of *Atonement*. As a film, it's superior to Nolan's effort, which – technically accomplished though it is – surrenders too often to crash-bang-wallop special effects and glorifies Dunkirk ahistorically.

The Dunkirk episode takes up fifty pages of the 370-page paperback edition of McEwan's book. *Atonement*'s larger narrative framework isn't directly to the point here, finely wrought though it is. It takes the form of a cat's-cradle play of fact and fiction, truth and lies, centred on a young working-class man, Robbie Turner, who is destined to rise in life having won a place at Cambridge University and patronage from his betters. His career is ended when he is falsely imprisoned for sexual molestation. His patrons stab him in the back. It is the old English story.

Released from prison, Robbie joins up days later and finds himself caught up in the Dunkirk retreat. As McEwan presents it, the evacuation is a shambles:

> He'd thought he had no expectations – until he saw the beach. He'd assumed that the cussed army spirit that whitewashed rocks in the face of annihilation would prevail. He tried to impose order now on the random movement before him, and almost succeeded: marshalling centres, warrant officers behind makeshift desks, rubber stamps and dockets, roped off lines towards waiting boats; hectoring sergeants, tedious queues around mobile canteens. Without knowing it, that was the beach he had been walking to for days. But the actual beach, the one he and the corporals gazed on now, was no more than a variation on all that had gone before: there was a rout, and this was its terminus. It was obvious enough now they saw it – this was what happened when a chaotic retreat could go no further.

'Chaotic' is the word, verging on 'surreal', with Zola's 'debacle' in the background. On his way to the beach, Robbie sees a leg, blown off by a bomb, resting snugly in the branches of a tree.

On the beach it is a total mess (no neat queues: Grenadiers here, Pioneers over there). A fat soldier has stripped off his khakis and is sunbathing. Not to spoil the story, Robbie's Dunkirk experience is not, ultimately, happy. Nor was McEwan's Dunkirk what Nolan represents.

McEwan had the advantage of eyewitness evidence about what Dunkirk was really like. In a *Paris Review* interview, he revealed that he had given his father – who had served and been wounded during the evacuation – a 'cameo' in *Atonement*: 'A dispatch rider from the Highland Light Infantry came by on a Norton. His bloodied legs dangled uselessly, and his pillion passenger, who had heavily bandaged arms, was working the foot pedals.' It was, apparently, McEwan's father who had the leg injuries, and the strange tandem partnership actually happened.

An RAF man on the beach is beaten to death by enraged Army men in McEwan's version because there are no Spitfires or Hurricanes in the air to protect the milling thousands of foot soldiers. The main strand of Nolan's film follows a heroic Spitfire pilot, and it is built up into the finale when, in order to keep fighting the Luftwaffe, the pilot exhausts the fuel in his tanks and crash-lands on the beach (aeronautically impossible). He sustains no risk of being beaten to death.

McEwan's debacle has the authority of his father's personal witness. His description is borne out by the thoughtful BBC television programme *Dunkirk*. What saved Britain was Hitler's spending valuable time quarrelling with his generals and thus holding back the Wehrmacht's tanks, which would have made short work of 380,000 British soldiers without any anti-tank weaponry. They were sitting ducks, fish in a barrel. Dunkirk would have been Britain's Stalingrad.

Hitler evidently held the crazed belief that he could do to England what he would do to Vichy: conquer and occupy by grudging proxy without spilling any Aryan blood. In short, what we 'remember' about Dunkirk is largely mythology. Nolan's film, wonderful cinema though it is, buys into that myth and propagates it, artistically. So by all means do what Brexit's guru Farage instructs – see the film – but weigh it carefully.

McEwan's Objection

I an McEwan is gifted, but also the most interestingly cross-grained of novelists currently dominating British fiction. As a writer he is always feeling for the frontiers of his craft. And, in a corner of his remarkable mind, he has passionately contrarian views about Brexit.

In March 2017 McEwan was reported in the broadsheet newspapers as having described 'the decision to hold a referendum on Brexit as reminiscent of Nazi Germany', and likening 'politicians and newspapers who attack judges scrutinising the process to Robespierre during the terror of the French Revolution'. The remarks were reportedly made in Barcelona, on a promotional tour for his latest novel, *Nutshell*.[111] In comments subsequently reported by Spanish newspapers (principally *El País*, the Spanish paper of record) and picked up by websites, McEwan described Brexit as 'a real disaster':

> Sixteen million Britons wanted to ſtay in the EU and 17 million wanted to leave, but there exiſts a small and very energetic political group made up of opaque and impatient people who are driving the process and who speak as though half the country were the entire country . . . It's also serious because Great Britain works on the basis of a parliamentary democracy and not through plebiscites, which remind me of the Third Reich . . .

[Brexit's] militant wing, the tabloid press, has started to look into the lives of the judges who rule that Brexit could result in the loss of human rights to see whether they're homosexual or something. It's reminiscent of Robespierre and the terror of the French Revolution. The air in my country is very foul.

McEwan was clearly thinking of the *Daily Mail*'s front-page headline 'Enemies of the People' from November 2016 attacking the Supreme Court, which determined that Article 50 be debated in the House of Commons before being dispatched to start the exit wheels rolling.

McEwan used *The Guardian* to 'clarify' his remarks a day or two later: 'I do not think for a moment', he said, 'that those who voted to leave the EU, or their representatives, resemble Nazis. Nor does our government even faintly resemble the Third Reich.' But manifestly the air still smelled foul to him. If nothing else, what this episode revealed was the extraordinary passion the whole Brexit episode had whipped up in the UK. It resembled, for a few months at least, civil war without gunfire.

Hail Hilary!

The most listened-to radio news programme in the UK is the BBC's three-hour early-morning feature *Today*. It was particularly well listened to on 29 March 2017, 'Article 50 Day', the day the die was cast. That day the historian David Starkey occupied the plum spot in the programme, 8.10 to 8.30. The audience crests to an average seven million Britons in those twenty minutes on good todays – or bad todays, as the millions of 'Remoaner' Britons might have thought the 29th was (the Ides of March came to mind). A ferociously outspoken Leaver,

Starkey took up a simple theme. This is the second time round, he explained, as if to History 101 in a less prestigious institution than his LSE. One pictured seven million ignoramuses craning towards their sets for instruction, dribbling their Weetabix and Nescafé.

The Brexit divorce, Starkey said, was a rerun of Old Copper-nose's split from Rome in the sixteenth century. As it happened, the seven million knew something about that historical rupture because they, and millions more, had watched the *Wolf Hall* miniseries on BBC TV in January and February 2015. It was an earlier, and more civil, history lesson for the nation.

Starkey, never one to mince his words and preferring, if stopped in his flow, to mince his interlocutor, brooked no interruption from twittering *Today* presenters as he thundered remorselessly on:

> We've of course been here before, this is only the second Brexit. We had a first and much bigger one that was the break with the Roman Catholic church under Henry VIII. And unlike the intolerably tedious conversation we've just had, they knew what they were doing, which was I think what the great bulk of the British people knew what they were doing in the referendum.

He hammered his words into the eardrums of his listeners. No tedium from Dr Starkey.

Nick Robinson, charged with maintaining political balance on his programme, mildly intervened: 'I invite you on this show and you attack . . .', but he never finished his sentence. He was cut off with the stern instruction: 'Shut up Nick and listen to somebody who actually knows something!' Robinson, an Oxford graduate, might have thought he knew some little things.

Today was rarely this entertaining. Henry VIII, Starkey repeated, had restored English independence 'in ways which are astonishingly similar to Brexit'. Not yet finished, he went on to compare the 'moaning Remainer' Nick Clegg with Sir Thomas More. Both had resisted the will of the (English) people. It cost More his head; the cosmopolitan Clegg (master of four European languages) might be lucky enough to get off with a bollocking on *Today*.

Asked what was the best on-screen drama about Henry VIII, most British viewers would see it as a toss-up between *Wolf Hall* and the 1966 adaptation of Robert Bolt's play *A Man for All Seasons*.[112] They take radically different views on the great Remainer, More, and the great Divorcer (from wives and from Rome), Henry, and his cunning factotum Thomas Cromwell, who will bend whichever way the wind is blowing.

Hilary Mantel has won the Booker Prize twice for the two first instalments of her Thomas Cromwell chronicles (*Wolf Hall* of 2009 is the first; the second is *Bring Up the Bodies*, 2012). In her second acceptance speech, she quipped: 'you wait twenty years for a bus then two come along at once'. It was sweetly said and her prize richly deserved.

Since more people saw the BBC TV version of *Wolf Hall* than had read the book (bestselling though it was), it's relevant to concentrate on one telling scene in Peter Kosminsky's adaptation, of which Mantel is said to have approved. The third instalment opens in 1531. The camera lingers a minute or two in close-up on the face of Thomas More – now Lord Chancellor of England – reading out Latin with the ease of someone for whom it is a first language. His features are composed and serene; he is a man at peace with himself and the world.

An abrupt shift across the room. We see something new and horrifying: a man is being put to the rack. He groans as the wheel is turned. It is Thomas Cromwell's barrister, James Bainham, who has gone over to the heretic Bible 'Englisher' Tyndale and cannot 'unbelieve' what the Ur-Protestant Tyndale teaches, even as his joints crack.

But is it Bainham or his master, Cromwell, who is More's target? The Lord Chancellor has used his office to intercept certain letters to the heretic Tyndale. More believes Cromwell to be a man whose 'faith is for purchase'. It is he who should be racked and cracked, and Tyndale, the man who dared to 'English' the Bible, burned at the stake (which he eventually was).

The prelude to the 'Great Matter' – English independence from Rome – is the Parliamentary Bill that will implement it. It's a document that More, as Chancellor, fatefully, declines to sign.[113] It will cost him not merely his office but his head, as he well knows.

It is impossible to know what influence Mantel had on the Brexit vote sixteen months later, but I suspect it was considerable. If only to make Starkey's point – it's all a rerun. *Wolf Hall*, on page and on screen, explored, with the sensitivity only great fiction can apply, the moral and psychological complexities of 'breaking away' and the fallacies of the 'clean break' myth. The novel handles all the issues in play with the delicacy of a juggler juggling soap bubbles. But when not a novelist, Mantel has very firm views.

But do they matter? The novel is what matters. Belittlingly, Starkey sees Mantel as a historical novelist, not a historian, a purveyor of 'total fiction'. *Wolf Hall* was, in his estimation, a 'deliberate perversion', fiction gone corrupt.

The alleged pervert did not take the attack lying down. It emerged that she was as fervent for Remain as was Starkey for Leave. On the day after Article 50's 'Dear John' to Brussels, and Starkey's history lesson to the nation, Mantel launched a scathing counter-attack. She started at the top. The country was being misled by a woman 'who was until recently famous only for her shoes', and who changed her convictions (Remain/ Leave, Leave/Remain) as regularly as her footwear.

Mantel prophesied that 'The liberal whimper will soon be drowned by complaint, as the results of Brexit and the results of "austerity" combine: job security gone, low pay endemic, justice beyond the average pocket, housing unaffordable, social care broken.' We shall see. It's an interesting time to be alive. And you don't have to agree with great novels to relish their greatness. I hope Mantel gets a third bus with the completion of her Cromwelliad.

The Satanic Verses: 'Not English!'

I have chosen to end with Salman Rushdie's novel *The Satanic Verses* (1988). It is probably not a book every Brexiteer reaches for, but Rushdie is exemplary in the Brexit debate. Born in Bombay, he is first-generation British, educated at an English public school and at Cambridge University. He is also a denizen (Muslim by original faith) of both India and Pakistan; he has been knighted by the Queen, and since 2000 he has lived in the USA. Among his remarkable achievements, Rushdie has globalized fiction.

After the furore about *The Satanic Verses* (initially by his British co-religionists, who burned it on a stake, in lieu of its author, then internationally with a fatwa from Ayatollah Khomeini), he was protected in 'safe houses' by order of Margaret Thatcher, who was satirized in the novel as 'Mrs Torture'. No writer's career, and writing, has been more wilfully paradoxical or self-definitional.

Rushdie is, pivotally, the focus of much of the ideological confusion of our time, particularly that connected with Brexit. His personal view was expressed pungently in a tweet the day after the referendum: 'Old Farts 1 The Future 0. Well done England.' (Rushdie is a Tottenham fan.) In an interview before the launch of his novel *The Golden House* (2017), he declared, with the air of a man saying 'farewell Albion':

I still have a deep attachment to England but when I visit now it feels like there's denial on all sides about what is going to happen after Brexit. Everyone is persuading themselves that it's going to be fine but it's obvious that it is not going to be fine. It feels like a country having a picnic on a railway track.

One supposes that most knights of the realm have a deep attachment to England.

Rushdie is a brilliant novelist who gets scathing reviews from a literary culture for whom a little magic realism (whatever that may be when it's at home) goes an awful long way. He has, despite these cavils, won not merely the Booker for *Midnight's Children* but the Booker of Bookers – an award hailing the novel as the best of British. End of.

The Satanic Verses is, primarily and controversially, a medita-tion on the Quran. It's not a subject that traditionally grips the Great British Public. The transcriber and falsifier of the sacred text is called Salman. But the novel begins with an event that is more directly relevant to the current Brexit crisis. Prophetic, even. A hijacked Air India jumbo jet (named after one of the gardens of Paradise) explodes in the air. Two subcontinentals fall 29,002 feet, the height of Everest, on to Hastings' shore – that historic beach where William the Conqueror ate his symbolic mouthfuls of sand before gobbling up the whole country. The newcomers are, miraculously, uninjured.

Gibreel Farishta and Saladin Chamcha are, as was William, illegal immigrants, or angel and devil, both of Muslim origin but Gibreel a film star who plays Hindu deities. Christian resurrection, and the fall of Satan, is also invoked: "'To be born again," sang Gibreel Farishta tumbling from the heavens, "first you have to die.'"

Relevant here is the excursus on that first and most dominant illegal immigrant, 'William the Conk'. Looking from her window on to the beach, an old, cognitively impaired woman sees the two immigrants land. They are, she thinks, the ghosts of Norman invaders. She has long been waiting for them:

I know what a ghost is, the old woman affirmed silently. Her name was Rosa Diamond; she was eighty-eight years old; and she was squinting beakily through her salt-caked bedroom windows, watching the full moon's sea. And I know what it isn't, too, she nodded further, it isn't scarification or a flapping sheet, so pooh and pish to all that bunkum. What's a ghost? Unfinished business, is what. – At which the old lady, six feet tall, straight-backed, her hair hacked short as any man's, jerked the corners of her mouth downwards in a satisfied, tragedy-mask pout, – pulled a knitted blue shawl tight around bony shoulders, – and closed, for a moment, her sleepless eyes, to pray for the past's return. Come on, you Norman ships, she begged: let's have you, Willie-the-Conk ... The coastline had changed, had moved a mile or more out to sea, leaving the first Norman castle stranded far from water, lapped now by marshy land that afflicted with all manner of dank and boggy agues the poor who lived there on their whatstheword estates ... Nine hundred years! Nine centuries past, the Norman fleet had sailed right through this Englishwoman's home.

On clear nights when the moon was full, she waited for its shining, revenant ghost ... Once as a girl on Battle

Hill, she was fond of recounting, always in the same time-polished words, – once as a solitary child, I found myself, quite suddenly and with no sense of ſtrangeness, in the middle of a war. Longbows, maces, pikes. The flaxen-Saxon bows, cut down in their sweet youth. Harold Arroweye and William with his mouth full of sand.

The clairvoyant Rosa takes the two illegal immigrants in, but Neighbourhood Watch has reported them. Fifty-seven immigration officers (beans in a can) mount a raid on Rosa's cottage. What was Samuel Beckett's consolation or warning from St Augustine? 'Do not despair, one of the thieves was saved. Do not presume one of the thieves was damned.' Transpose 'immigrants' for thieves. Look at those pathetic makeshift boats bringing refugees to Europe – are they to be damned or saved? If TM/ PM achieves her 100,000 immigration figure, what happens to number 100,001? Damned or saved?

Rushdie's contention is that, like it or not, vote as you will, England in the future will be conditioned – defined, even – by the immigrants who come here. Those millions (now billions) of feet are tramping towards us. If the incomers achieve what their laureate Rushdie has achieved for 'English' fiction, it's a happy prospect. Or, perhaps, we shall be 'swamped', as Thatcher/ Torture put it. Time will tell.

Epilogue

Over the months I've been writing this book, the Brexit road has redirected 'Your England, My England' as fundamentally as did the Norman Conquest, the Reformation, the Reform Acts of 1832 and 1867, the female emancipations of 1917 and 1928, and the welfare state legislation of the post-war period.

It has been stimulating, against this background, to reread 'English' literature (or revealing particles of its continental mass) through a Brexit optic. Many of the issues on which UKIP defines itself are mulled over, this way and that, in our great books. It's unsurprising, when one thinks of it. What goes around comes around: from Byrhtnoth in the mud and William on the Hastings sand, to Gibreel Farishta falling to life-in-death on Britain's coast.

Of course, the reverberations of this great change in what England/Britain/the UK is becoming will, in years to come, find further literary expression. Ezra Pound called great writers the antennae of the race, and he was right. It's an interesting time to be alive – and reading.

REFERENCES

1   See Disraeli's *Sybil, or The Two Nations* (1845). Disraeli's 'One Nation' conservatism is routinely evoked at annual party conferences.

2   Nietzsche's assertion, in *The Antichrist*, is that the Cross is not an argument.

3   I have recently reviewed for the *New York Times*, with hearty approval for its thesis, Martin Puchner's *The Written World: How Literature Shaped Civilization* (New York, 2017).

4   It vexed Spender mightily if one called it a tapestry. Neither is the Bayeux hanging, properly speaking, a tapestry, but an embroidery.

5   I.e. leader. Chiefs, like husbands, gave rings to the most loyal of their followers. See the exquisite Anglo-Saxon poem 'The Seafarer', recorded in the tenth-century Exeter Book.

    The passage quoted tells us how Byrhtnoth raises his spear and shield and vauntingly defies the invader (who can see but not hear him). He tells the Danes' messenger (who has brought the peremptory demand to submit and pay, as usual) to return to his heathen masters. The bill will not be paid this year. Byrhtnoth ends, scornfully, that it would be a pity for them to have come so far and not have a battle. Let battle commence.

6   The term 'carpetbaggers' originated with the Union administrators who carried carpet bags (travelling bags) to 'reconstruct' the South, after the American Civil War. They were hated.

7   Perhaps more symbolic than historic. There is even some doubt that Harold was killed by an arrow in the eye, as portrayed in the Bayeux Tapestry. Legend is often stronger than fact.

8   The name means 'Final Judgment Book'. Only God, when he descended at the end of days, could countermand it.

9   The Normans also invaded Ireland, and created an English 'lordship' over the land in 1169. There is a pretty congruity in the DUP supporting the maimed Theresa May on her way to Brexit in 2017.

10 See Tony Palmer's film *England, My England* (1995), celebrating that most English of composers, Henry Purcell.

11 Simply search for 'red cross tattoo' online to get a veritable gallery of chesty variations.

12 See W. M. Thackeray's series in *Punch*, 'Novels by Eminent Hands' (1847). Bulwer-Lytton's hand was more eminent than most – he was a baronet, and made sure his readers knew it.

13 The reference is to the comic travesty of English history as taught in schools *1066 and All That* (1930), by W. C. Sellar and R. J. Yeatman. It is delightful, relaxed reading for the Brexiteer, and divides its chronicle into 'good things' and 'bad things'.

14 See George MacDonald Fraser, *The Hollywood History of the World* (London, 1988). More about Fraser later, vis-à-vis Flashman.

15 Or of having your bowels 'liquefied' by an enemy spear, an alternative and perhaps more plausible account of Harold's death at Hastings.

16 The Good Brexiteer will, of course, lament the fact that the 'Chunnel' (Channel Tunnel) no longer terminates at Waterloo station.

17 Brooke chose the Shakespearian sonnet form for this poem, not the Petrarchan, to add a patriotic grace note.

18 In 1848–9 Bulwer-Lytton (again) wrote the Malory-inspired epic *King Arthur*, which he called 'the grand effort of my literary life'.

19 See P.J.C. Field, *Romance and Chronicle: A Study of Malory's Prose Style* (London, 1971).

20 For more on this quintessentially English directory, see 'DNB/OED'.

21 *Morte d'Arthur*, for example, is most readily read, with three or four mouse clicks, on Project Gutenberg, free of charge: www.gutenberg.org.

22 I read on 30 November 2017 that President Macron intends French to take over as the world language, now that the UK is leaving the EU. Some hopes, *mon brave*.

23 An echo of his biblical peer, Solomon: 'Comfort me with apples: for I am sick of love' (Song of Solomon 2:5).

24 Hence, in Orwell's *Nineteen Eighty-four* (1949), for example, the Party's great effort is to primitivize the English language for the people into 'Newspeak' – a few hundred words. The Party will, of course, retain ownership of the whole range of English words (Oldspeak).

25 Details are laid out at more length in Green's Wikipedia entry.

26 See, again, the Wikipedia entry on Dominic Chappell.

27 As reported in *The Guardian*, 26 April 2016.

28 The result was 66.3 per cent Leave, 33.6 per cent Remain. In early 2017 Sir [still 'Sir'] Philip Green agreed to kick in £360 million to the BHS pension fund. Chappell went on trial in August 2017. They went for the sprat not the whale, as Frank Field MP sardonically noted.

29 Battered with the hard dints of martyrdom and persecution that previous generations had suffered for their Christian faith.

30 The red-cross flag, the insignia of St George, became universal on English soldiers' battledress as early as the fourteenth century. Scotland has always displayed the St Andrew's cross.

31 'Boadicea' is the romanized name given by Tacitus to the Iceni queen. Modern accounts go variously for Buduica, Boudicca or Buduica.

32 Buckingham. It is, as I say, a university that is defiantly independent of state funding.

33 Shakespeare, oddly, had no interest in the warrior queen. His erstwhile collaborator John Fletcher wrote a tragicomedy, *Bonduca*, judged feeble.

34 See Alan Kingston, *Boudicca: Warrior Queen* (London, 2003).

35 Graham Webster, *Boudicca: The British Revolt against Rome*, AD 60 (London, 1978).

36 The 'Gauls' are the above-mentioned Welsh insurgents.

37 The Roman name for Colchester.

38 In the following paragraphs I am indebted to Bruno Bettelheim, *The Uses of Entertainment* (London, 1976). The prince's unsanctioned kissing of the sleeping Snow White (did someone feed her Rohypnol?) was condemned as sexual assault by a critic in November 2017, with the demand that the story be dropped from the bedtime curriculum.

39 I take this figure, which seems rather high to me, from Wikipedia.

40 'British' not 'English', because Lear is king of what is now the UK, not a region of it.

41 The late 1590s is the best date for the composition of the play. Shakespeare, one might surmise, was pondering in his mind the uncertainties of what would happen after Elizabeth.

42 Something that Josephine Tey anticipated in her brilliant detective novel *The Daughter of Time* (1951).

43 I have gone into this in detail in my puzzle book (written with Cedric Watts) *Is Henry V a War Criminal?* (Oxford, 2001).

44 The founder of the school was the famous Elizabethan actor Edward Alleyn.

45 Ted Jeory, 'Farage's Fascist Past? Nigel Boasted about his NF Initials and Sang "Gas Them All", Claims Schoolfriend', *The Independent*, 11 August 2016, www.independent.co.uk.

46 Jack Elam, about whom I wrote in *The Boy Who Loved Books* (2007), was the most intellectually cultivated schoolteacher I have ever known.

47 Recall, for example, the 'I'm backing Britain' campaign in the 1960s.

48 I deal with the writing of this novel in *Victorian Novelists and Publishers* (Chicago, IL, 1976).

49 A slight fib. I first came across it as a Classic Comic, then read it properly.

50 *The Sun*'s headline of 4 April 2017, echoing the paper's immortal 'Up Yours Delors' of 1990.

51 One suspects that John Fowles, author of *The French Lieutenant's Woman* (1969), knew *Westward Ho!*

52 See, for example, her poem 'On Monsieur's Departure'. The historians' consensus is that Elizabeth did indeed write the Tilbury Address. It is more authentically hers than Donald Trump's teleprompter-dictated podium speeches are his. The illiterate tweets are something else entirely.

53 John Bagot Glubb, *The Fate of Empires and the Search for Survival* (Edinburgh, 1978).

54 Ozymandias is another name for Rameses II. He was the greatest builder of all the Egyptian pharaohs and indeed did leave great statues of himself. The newer mighty of the world take not the slightest notice of them.

55 The Wolseley, in Piccadilly (when I can afford it, which is seldom).

56 First called *Susan*, it entered the world as *Northanger Abbey* in 1817, one of her last published works.

57 See the word 'comfort' in the First Shepherd's outburst in the Wakefield Mystery play, above. I also see a connection with Orwell's reverence for English 'gentleness', below.

58 'Culture' here means agriculture, English farming, as opposed to wild verdure, greenery.

59 See Helena Kelly, *Jane Austen: Secret Radical* (New York, 2016).

60 For the record, Austen's county voted 55 per cent for Brexit; Gosport, her nearby town, a whopping 64 per cent.

61 In *The Wild Duck* (1884), a study of self-deluding mythopoeia.

62 See Christopher Hope, 'Nigel Farage and Enoch Powell: The Full Story of UKIP's Links with the "Rivers of Blood" Politician', *The Telegraph*, 12 December 2014, www.telegraph.co.uk.

63 Farage received less than 1,000 votes.

64 See 'Shakespeare: "This England"'. More closely Kipling is alluded to.

65 Patrick Hennessey, 'David Cameron Backs Jerusalem as English National Anthem', *The Telegraph*, 14 July 2012, www.telegraph.co.uk.

66 Cristina Odone, 'Nigel Farage: We Must Defend Christian Heritage', *The Telegraph*, 1 November 2013, www.telegraph.co.uk.

67 That bookcase is probably already groaning, so both resources are available online. The dnb was revised in the 1990s as the ODNB (*The Oxford Dictionary of National Biography*).

68 Raymond Williams argued that the OED was the only resource, other than literature itself, that a literary critic needed. His book for the desert island, perhaps. See his *Keywords* (New York and London, 1976).

69 The gender imbalance is corrected in the ODNB, although it is hampered by the fact that men are memorialized more than women. Do a count of the obituaries in your favoured newspaper. In mine it runs two-to-one, male over female.

1975; revd edn 2002), p. 54. I draw on Sutcliffe in my account of the oED

Peter Sutcliffe, *The Oxford University Press: An Informal History* (Oxford, 1975; revd edn 2002), p. 54. I draw on Sutcliffe in my account of the OED and DNB.

Edward Greenfield, 'The Shortlived Proms Ban on Land of Hope and

71 Edward Greenfield, 'The Shortlived Proms Ban on Land of Hope and Glory – Archive' [6 June 1969], *The Guardian*, 7 September 2016, www.theguardian.com.

72 See 'Elgar Navy', 3 August 2004, at http://boyntonesque.blogspot.co.uk. See also David C. F. Wright, 'Elgar Unmasked', n.d., at www.wrightmusic. net/pdfs/elgar/pdf.

73 Orwell's mother was half-French, a fact about him that is characteristically overlooked.

74 One of the motives of that foggy war was the fear that other sources of gold ore were running out.

75 See Nigel Biggar, 'Rhodes, Race and the Abuse of History', *Standpoint*, March 2016, www.standpointmag.co.uk.

76 See Amit Chaudhuri, 'The Real Meaning of Rhodes Must Fall', *The Guardian*, 16 March 2016, www.theguardian.com.

77 See www.youtube.com. The video, posted by 'YouKipper', had 13,722 hits at the time of writing.

78 His defiance echoes the comedian Bob Monkhouse's joke: 'They all laughed when I said I wanted to be a comedian. Well, they're not laughing now.'

79 His favourite poem was George Meredith's 'The Lark Ascending', as enhanced by Ralph Vaughan Williams's musical depiction.

80 Buchan had cut his teeth, professionally, as an administrator in South Africa at a period when the spirit of Rhodes was riding high.

81 *Jumbo: The Unauthorised Biography of a Victorian Sensation* (London, 2013).

82 An article in *The Guardian* in 2017 reported that the British aristocracy, numerically tiny, still owned a third of the British land mass. Chris Bryant, 'How the Aristocracy Preserved their Power', *The Guardian*, 7 September 2017, www.theguardian.com.

83 See Lawrence's poetry collection *Look! We Have Come Through!* (1917), particularly the opening 'Argument'.

84 The phrase was originated by Thomas Carlyle, discussing 'social problem' fiction of the 1840s.

85 Amit Chaudhuri, 'Why the Romance of Brexit Bloomed in Philip Larkin's Industrial Suburbia', *The Guardian*, 8 August 2016, www. theguardian.com.

86 The picture is easily found through an online image search for 'Philip Larkin'.

87 She once told me they were both thinking of voting National Front, although I'm not sure she was serious. Leicester is the first city in England with a white minority. See Alice Philipson, 'White Britons a Minority in Leicester, Luton and Slough', *The Telegraph*, 10 January 2013, www.telegraph.co.uk.

88 Denis Staunton, 'London Letter: David Hockney a Rare Brexiteer among British Cultural Giants', *Irish Times*, 10 February 2017, www.irishtimes.com.

89 Alan Bennett, 'Postscript: 23 June 2016', in *Keeping On Keeping On* (London, 2016), quoted ibid.

90 The faux proverb was actually first produced by Kipling, in *Kim* (1901). It may have been current as small talk in hotter regions of the Empire.

91 The full lyrics, and a cinematic version of Coward singing them, can be found on YouTube.

92 He shares the nickname with the revered grand old man of Edwardian cricket, Sir Pelham ('Plum') Warner, whom Wodehouse must surely have seen play. He acknowledged the coincidence and was pleased by it. Wodehouse, a good fast bowler for Dulwich College, dreamed of being a cricketer, one is told. He came on the idea of Jeeves while watching Percy Jeeves play a good game of cricket.

93 Colin Dexter played the same trick with 'Endeavour' Morse. Detectives' identity, like that of butlers, is compressed into the surname – does anyone call Lestrade by his first name? Modern TV versions embarrassedly call him 'Greg'.

94 This delicately painful situation is handled brilliantly in the 1983 Merchant–Ivory film, with Anthony Hopkins playing Stevens.

95 Christopher Hope, 'Mass Immigration Has Left Britain "Unrecognisable", Says Nigel Farage', *The Telegraph*, 28 February 2014, www.thetelegraph.co.uk.

96 I. F. Clarke, *Voices Prophesying War: Future Wars, 1763–3749* (London and New York, 1966).

97 The Americanized film from 1953, produced by George Pal, is in my view best. I saw it five times in a week, aged fifteen, on its first release in Colchester, Essex.

98 The manuscript was turned down by 'at least' a dozen publishers, which says something about those entrusted with providing our reading matter.

99 'The Last Testament of Flashman's Creator: How Britain has Destroyed Itself', *Daily Mail*, 5 January 2008, www.dailymail.co.uk. The article was extracted from Fraser's last, non-fiction, book, *The Light's On at Signpost* (2002).

100 He was, the novels remind us, educated (as was Tony Blair) at Fettes, the country's leading public school. The former milkman Sean Connery, Scottish though he is, did not quite carry that off.

101 The excuse didn't wash with Ernő Goldfinger, an architect whose family had been forced into exile by the Nazis. He took legal action, which proved an embarrassment to the novel and its creators.

102 The website was named after its pioneering, short-lived founder, Andrew Breitbart.

103 'Virgil', 'Decline and Fall: The Grim Message of the Camp of the Saints', *Breitbart News*, 24 November 2014, www.breitbart.com.

104 It's hard not to recall Danny Boyle's pageant inaugurating the 2012 London Olympics. Somewhere, Virginia Woolf must have been laughing.

105 This description is modified from the entry on the novel in my *How to Be Well Read* (London, 2013).

106 This description is modified from the entry on the novel in my *How to Be Well Read*.

107 The other two are *Money: A Suicide Note* (1984) and *The Information* (1995).

108 This description is an altered version of the entry on the novel in my *How to Be Well Read*.

109 The generic title for the British private soldier, 'Tommy Atkins', has been proverbial for at least three hundred years.

110 Some might nominate the American Paul Gallico's *The Snow Goose* (1940), which was written in the immediate aftermath (and before America entered the war). I find it too saccharine.

111 Sam Jones, 'I am McEwan: Referendums such as Brexit Vote Remind Me of Third Reich', *The Observer*, 12 March 2017. *Nutshell* is totally apolitical.

112 Charles Laughton's magnificent depiction of the king in *The Private Life of Henry* viii (1933) has been forgotten, with the generation who could never look at a chicken drumstick without wanting to throw it over their shoulder.

113 The document the British Parliament drew up in 2017 to legislate Britain's withdrawal from Europe was named, allusively, 'The Great Repeal Bill'.

ACKNOWLEDGEMENTS

I am grateful to Ben Hayes for suggesting the idea of this book. David Hayden and Aimee Selby have been encouraging and corrective editors and I am grateful to them. My greatest debt is to John Crace, the leading political wit of our time, for providing his introduction to this book and for what I have learned from him over many laughing lunches over many years.